Introduction

Football is the greatest game in the world. The reason for this is that almost anybody can play it, and it is simple enough for almost anybody to understand.

It is no coincidence that it is the most international game of them all — it breaks more language barriers than any other activity.

But even something as simple as football has to be taught. And that is the reason for this book.

Because there is nothing complicated about football, there is nothing complicated about this book. It sets out the basic ideas of football in a way that can be easily understood. It explains the basic skills and tactics, and it explains just how easy it is for any ambitious youngster to become proficient at the game.

Once the beginner has mastered the basic techniques, he will find like millions before him, that football can become a way of life. Indeed, for some it can become a rewarding profession.

First published 1974
Revised edition 1984
Second impression 1985
Published by Hamlyn Publishing,
a division of The Hamlyn Publishing Group Ltd,
Astronaut House, Hounslow Road,
Feltham, Middlesex, England

© Copyright 1974 The Hamlyn Publishing Group Limited

ISBN 0 600 38980 4
PRINTED IN BELGIUM
This book was originally entitled *My Learn to play Soccer*

My fun to play
Football

Illustrated by
Michael Jackson

HAMLYN

London · New York · Sydney · Toronto

Kicking

Kicking is the most neglected of the football arts for the reason that it is done so simply — or so everybody thinks. There would seem to be nothing to it: if you put your foot behind the ball, away it goes. And, as it is far more exciting dribbling or shooting, kicking is hardly ever practised.

But that outlook is mistaken. Kicking correctly is the basis of any skill, and without mastering the skills, you will never be more than just another footballer. If you want to be something special — and who doesn't? — then you must understand the basics of kicking, and know why, to make the ball perform certain functions, it is necessary to kick it in a certain manner.

It is not difficult, but practice can become boring. Nevertheless, all good footballers keep at it, and even First Division players spend a few minutes of each training session practising basics, making sure that they are striking the ball correctly, and that they are masters of the ball, rather than the other way round.

And what is good enough for international players is good enough for the rest of us.

Keep your weight over the ball!

RIGHT
This is the right way to kick a ball. The knee is bent well above the ball, and the instep is being used to combine maximum power with accuracy.

WRONG
Now, the wrong way: the balance has been lost because the body is too far back. Control has therefore gone, and a ball cannot be kicked hard with the toe.

MAKING A BALL SWERVE
Simply 'wipe' the kicking foot across the ball in the opposite direction to that in which you want it to go. To make the ball swerve to the right, hit it on the left side.

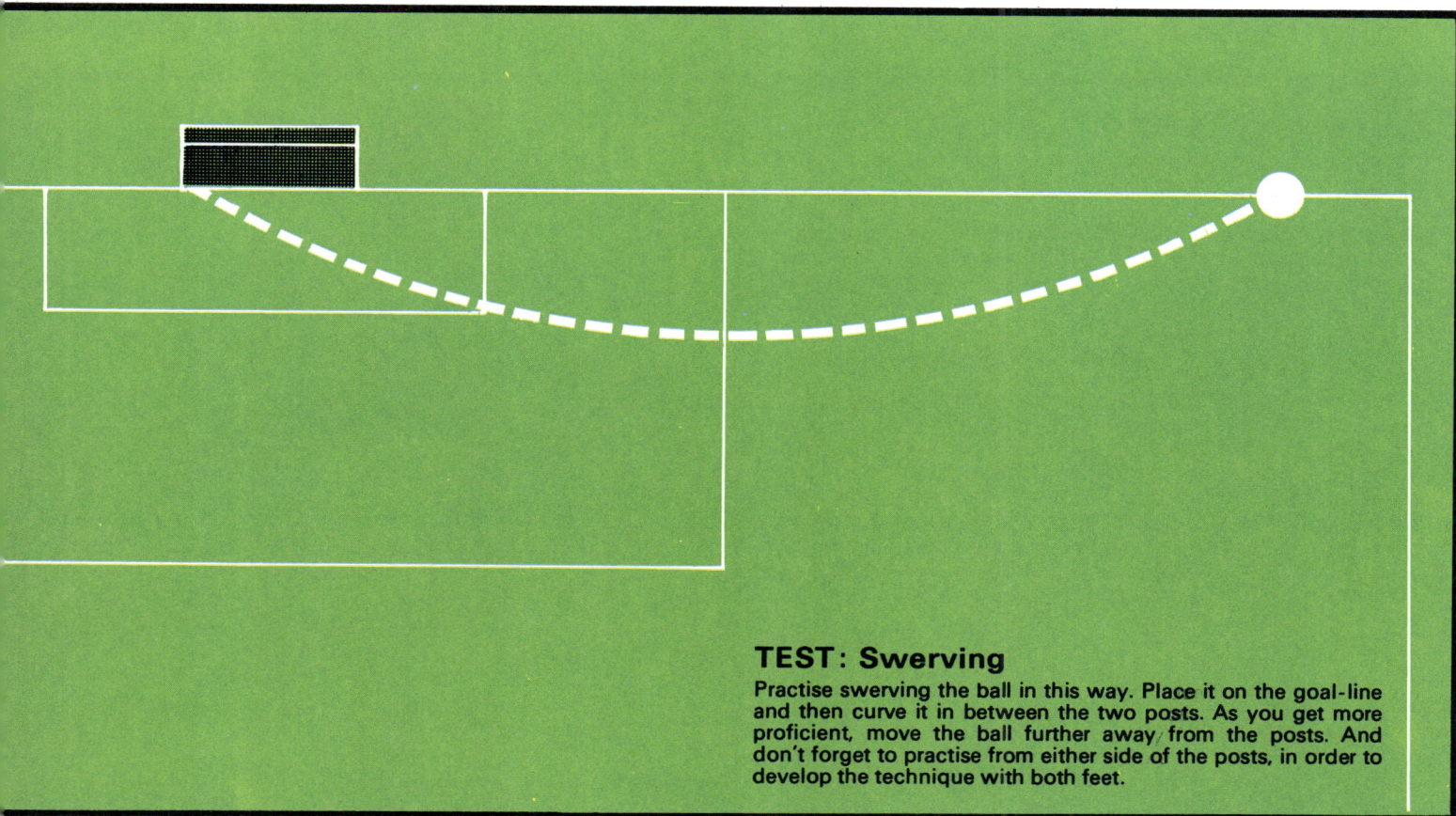

TEST: Swerving

Practise swerving the ball in this way. Place it on the goal-line and then curve it in between the two posts. As you get more proficient, move the ball further away from the posts. And don't forget to practise from either side of the posts, in order to develop the technique with both feet.

Diego Maradona of Argentina in action.

LOFTING THE BALL

There was once a famous coach who used to tell his pupils that football was played on the ground, and not in the air. Although he meant that skills with the feet are most important, don't fall into the trap of believing that it is a crime to kick the ball in the air. It isn't. Because when you think about it, 'upstairs' is often the safest place for the ball, particularly when you have to make a long pass. Obviously a long ball on the ground has a chance of being intercepted, but the ball that goes through the air has not.

Giving the ball some air, as the professionals say, is not difficult. Just remember to strike the ball as low down as you can, get as deep underneath it as possible, lean the body well back, and try to keep the non-kicking foot from getting level with the ball. But remember, the object of the exercise is to reach a team-mate. Height is not everything, you need distance as well. There is nothing to be gained just by kicking the ball as high as possible.

TEST

There is a simple way to develop this skill. Take a ball on to a pitch, and from about midway between the halfway line and the goal line, kick a ball into the goal. But drop it first bounce into the goal area before it passes between the posts. This will teach you the art of dropping the ball into a particular area. As your proficiency increases, lengthen the distance of your 'clearances' or passes by going back towards the halfway line. **See diagram 1.**

CHIPPING THE BALL

We have talked about lofting the ball as a method of beating two or three opponents through the air over a long distance. Chipping the ball is different, for it is used over a short distance. When you are sending a lofted pass over a distance, it does not normally matter if the ball bounces and goes rolling on. But with a chip you aim to put a little back-spin on the ball, to check the speed after it bounces.

Chipping is the ideal way to beat a defender when there is space behind him. A good chip into that space will check its pace on pitching, and will 'wait' for the attacker running on to it.

This is how it is done: the kicking foot has to be dug down into the ball, rather like an expert billiards player who puts 'stun' on the ball by striking down at the bottom. The knee of the kicking leg must be well bent, and the non-kicking foot placed slightly in front of the ball if possible. Chipping is certainly not easy. But it is a tremendously valuable technique to perfect.

TEST

Use the centre circle for practice. Stand about 20 metres from the centre spot and softly chip the ball up so that it bounces just inside the circle. If you have put the right amount of back-spin on it, the ball will slow up after pitching and stop before it can roll out of the opposite side of the circle. **See diagram 2.**

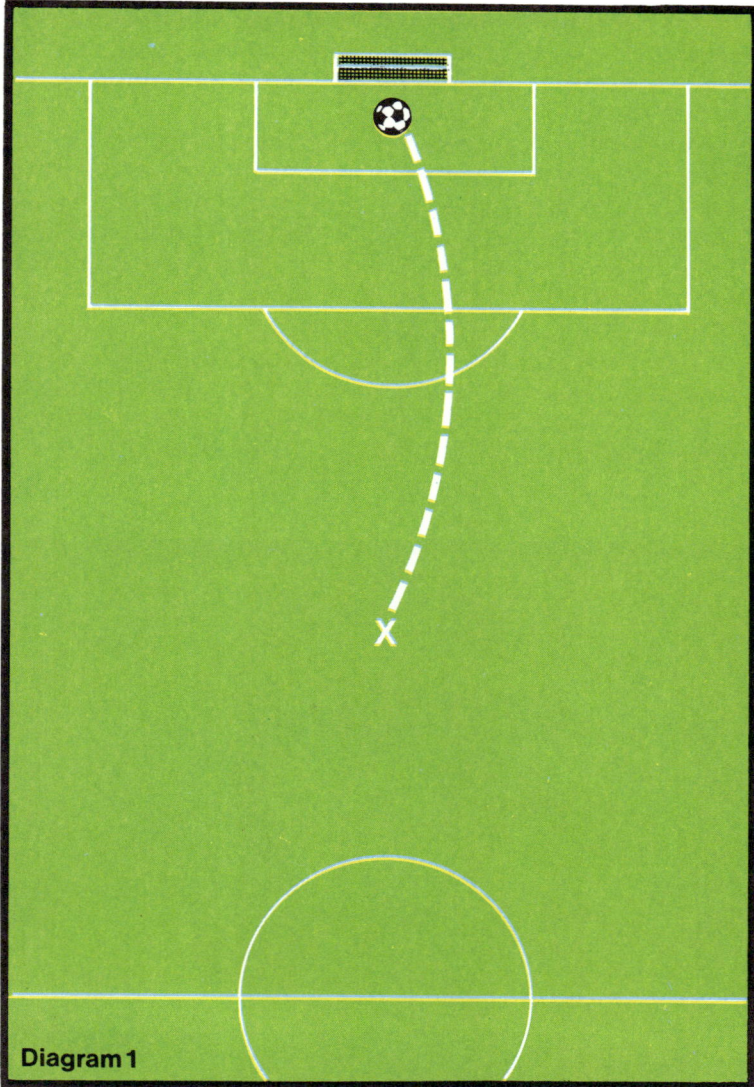

Diagram 1

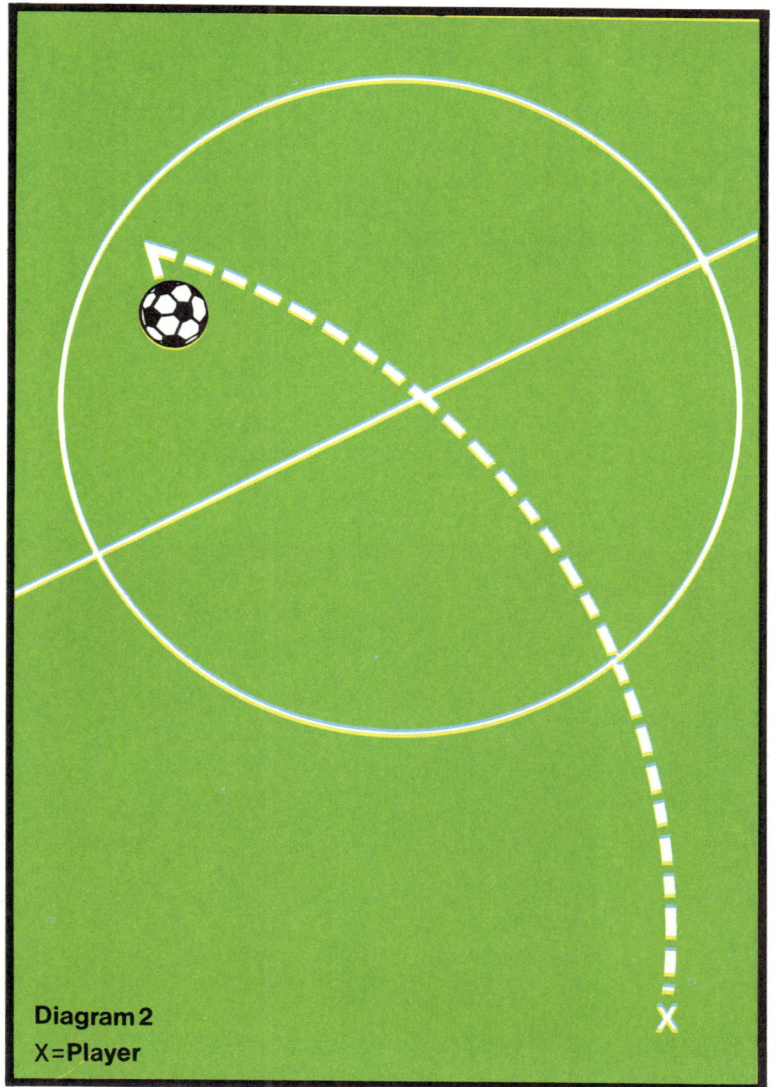

Diagram 2
X=Player

Schuster of West Germany demonstrating a chip.

Heading

You want to get into your school team, don't you? So consider the problem of the master choosing the team, when he is faced with two boys of equal ability on the ground. It does not take a genius to realise that the place in the team will be given to the lad who can be useful when the ball is in the air, does it?

That is why heading, which is too often neglected, is so important. Perhaps heading is neglected through a fear of getting hurt. There is no danger in heading a football so long as the correct part of the head, the *forehead*, is used.

The amount of confidence any player can acquire through being able to head a ball properly is tremendous. It is one of the most satisfying skills in the game.

Next time you watch an international match on television, or better still if you are lucky enough to be taken to see one, watch closely how the great players make use of their heads – you will be surprised how much they do that you had not noticed before, because it is done so skilfully and quietly that it is taken for granted.

See how quickly they can outwit the opposition, because they do not have to wait for the ball to come to the ground before they can use it. That is why heading is such a vital part of the game.

RIGHT

This is the right way to head a ball. Hit it with the forehead, try and keep your eyes open as long as possible, and don't only use your neck — brace your shoulders as well.

WRONG

There is nothing dangerous about heading a football. But if you use the top of the head, instead of the forehead, you will have no control over direction, and get a headache!

HEADING DOWN

The basic principles still apply. But time the impact so that the forehead is well over the top of the ball. You will find also that you get more power heading the ball that way.

HEADING TO THE SIDE

Not as difficult as it looks. Accuracy is more important than strength because normally the purpose of this type of header is just to direct the ball to a nearby colleague.

West Germany's Karl-Heinz Rummenigge beats his opponents in the 1982 World Cup finals.

TEST: Heading

Now here is a way to improve your heading ability, the way that the professionals use. Suspend a ball from a cross bar on the end of a piece of rope, letting it hang at head height. In this exercise your feet stay on the ground. There is no jumping.

Right? Here we go. Head the ball outwards. As it comes back, head it again to the right. Head to the right again, and again, and again until you can turn a full circle keeping the ball in play all the time. Repeat the test turning to the left. This drill will teach you to head, with emphasis on control.

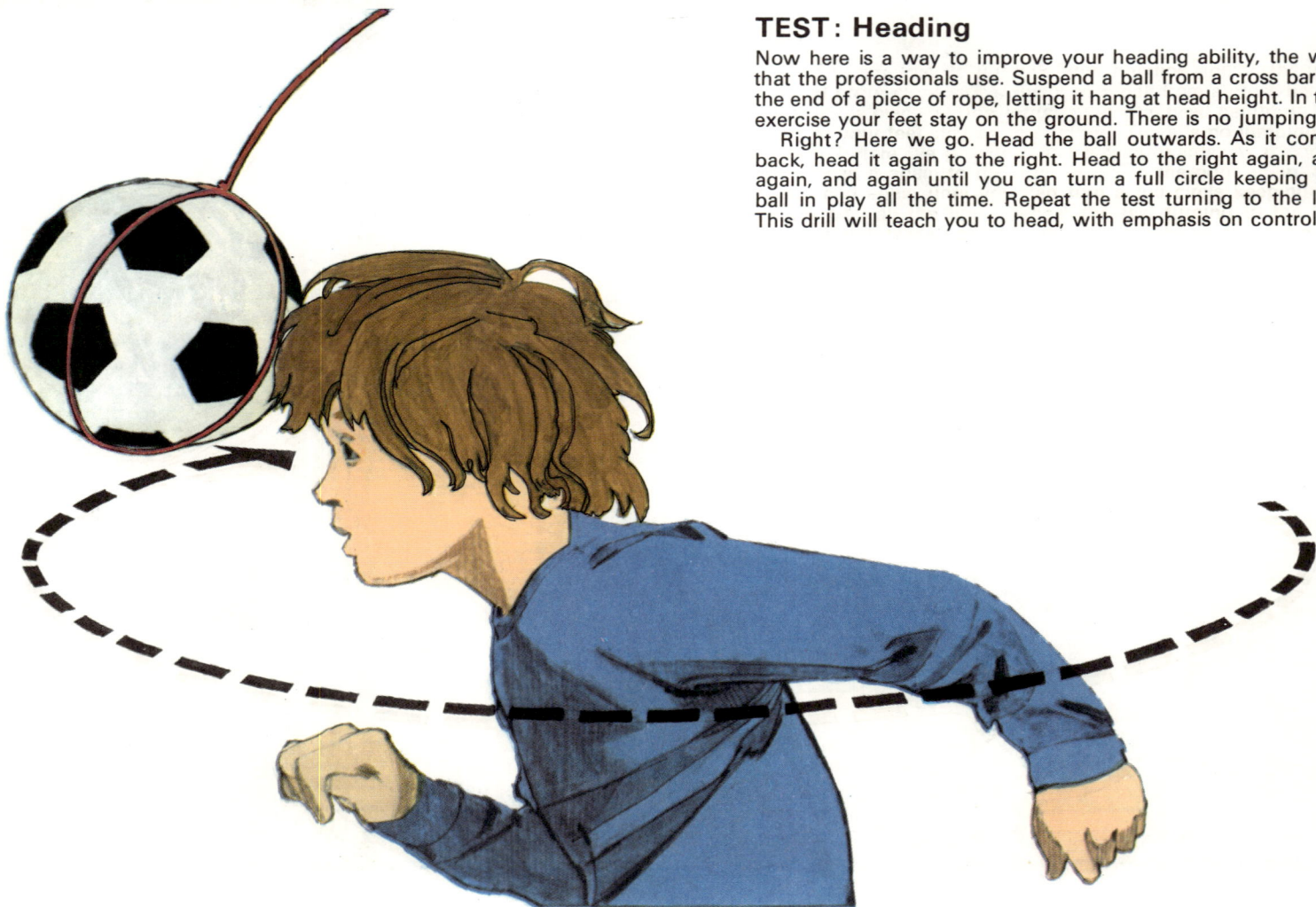

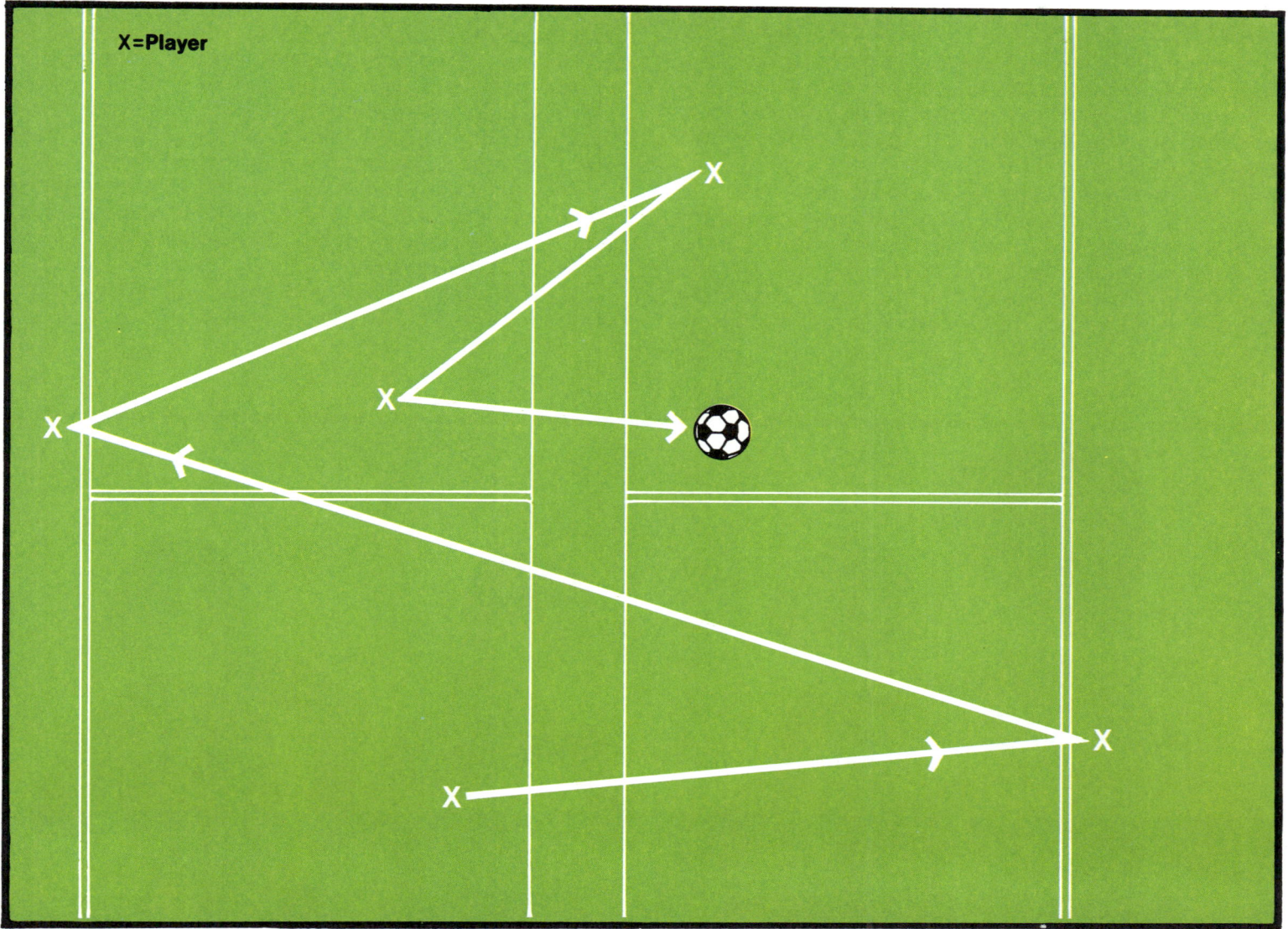

X=Player

HEAD TENNIS

You can play exactly as the diagram suggests, with one, two, three, four or five players either side of the net or rope: the marking can be optional. You lose a point each time you do not get it back after the first bounce. Score as in tennis — or whichever way you like.

Control and passing

We would all like to be another Bobby Charlton or Norman Whiteside, producing a shot that can blast a hole right through the net. But while that ability is useful, to say the least, it is by no means the whole story.

Power is magnificent, even on its own. But it is power plus *control* that is the combination guaranteed to take any beginner towards the top.

When you listen to a top coach, he will tell you that possession of the ball is the most important part of the game . . . that when you are in posses-sion, no matter in which part of the field, then your side is attacking; and that when the other side has possession, then you must be on the defensive.

You see now how important it is to be able to control and to pass the ball well. If you can do both those things, then you are likely to be able to keep your team in possession.

But remember that the other side are not going to stand around and let you do it unchallenged. So, you must be able to control the ball and get it away to a colleague quickly.

Master these skills, and you will become the player most feared by the other side.

Power-speed-CONTROL!

Bobby Moore was famous for his ball control.

FOOT

Try and put your foot on top of the ball if you can. And take your time. Hurry, and the ball will bounce away from you.

CHEST

Make sure you do take the ball on your chest, and not on your stomach. Take the ball high on the breastbone and 'give' a little.

THIGH

To be used only when you have not got time to let the ball drop to your feet. But get the ball to the ground as quickly as possible.

Cerezo passing to his Brazilian team mate.

'WALL' PASS

This is the simplest and the safest way for two team-mates to beat one opponent. And it makes a lot more sense than the man with ball trying to dribble, and thereby risk losing the ball. Attacker B passes to Attacker A and, while the ball is on its way from B to A and back again, Attacker B runs round the opponent and collects the ball in the open space.

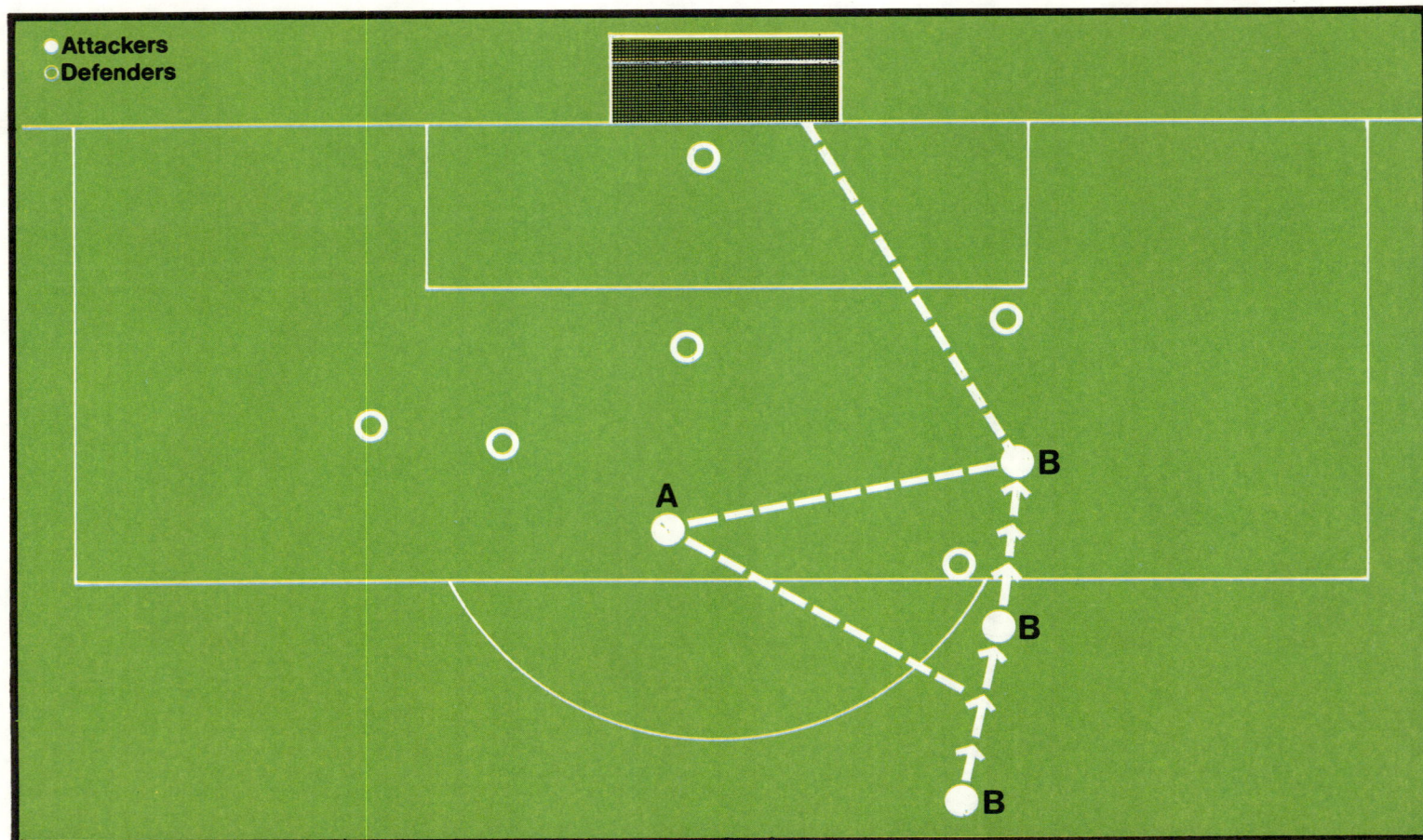

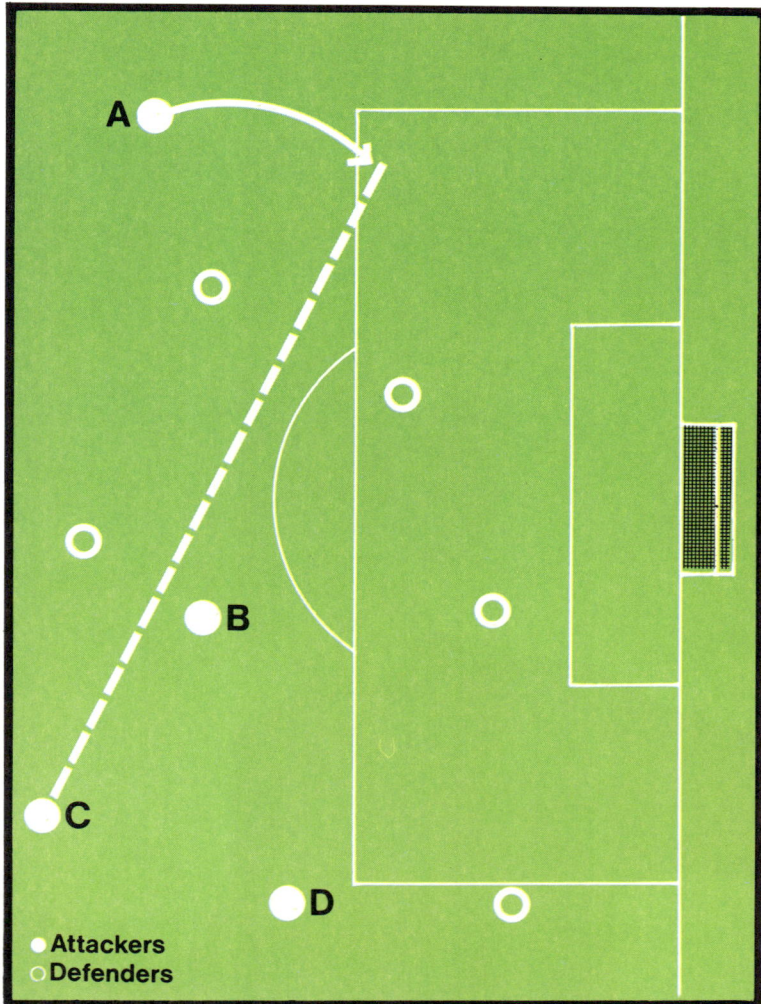

LEFT: THE LOFTED PASS

Attacker C advances with the ball. He has colleagues B and D near him, but there will still be opponents between them and the goal. So Attacker C has not beaten anybody. But if he lofts the ball over the heads of the defenders, then Attacker A has a clear run to goal.

TEST: Passing

Sharpen up your passing this way: find a brick wall and run along it flicking the ball against it with the outside of the left foot. Then come back using the outside of the right foot. The success of the exercise lies in performing it as fast as possible.

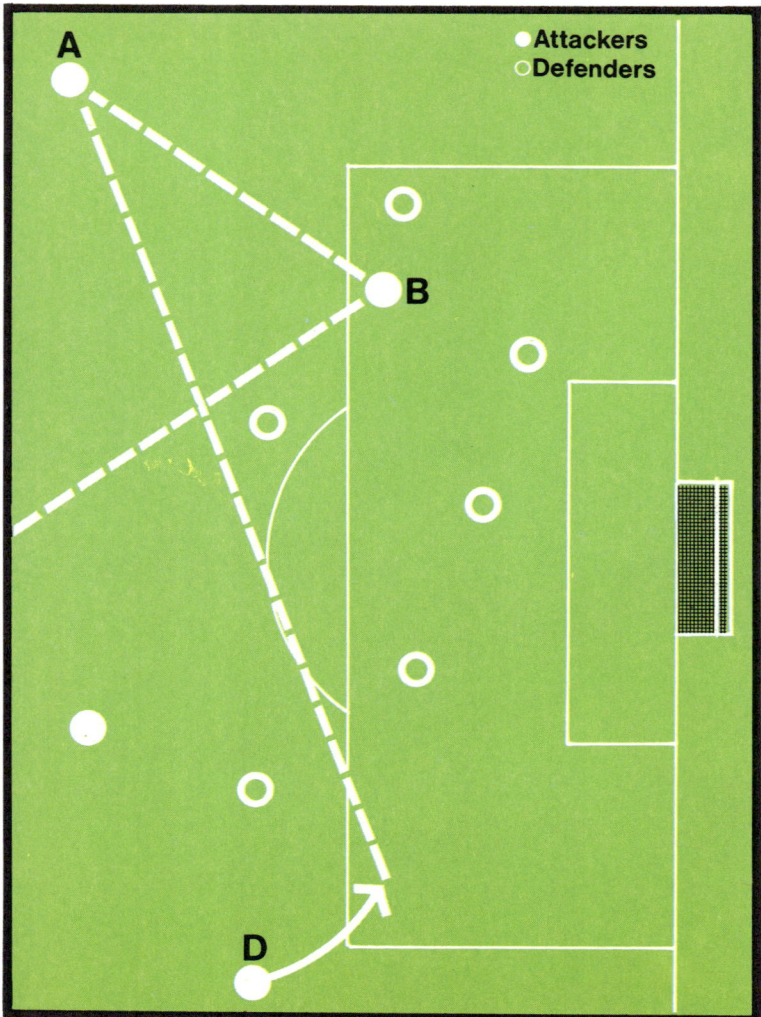

LEFT: WHEN TO PASS BACK

The ball is cleared upfield to Attacker B. But he has four defenders closing in. He has the sense not to try and beat them, but pushes the ball back to Attacker A, who hits it across the field to create a scoring chance for Attacker D.

Dribbling

Dribbling is a unique Soccer skill: the better the team for which you play, the less dribbling you are likely to do.

But when you start playing organised team football you will find yourself doing a lot of it for the simple reason that the players around you are not so skilful at playing 'off the ball'. That means they have not taken up positions which make it easy for the player with the ball to pass it to them. And that in turn means that the player with the ball has got to 'take on' opponents and beat them in what the professionals call a 'one-to-one' situation.

But even the professionals are unable to do it all according to the text-book, and the ability to dribble is an absolute must if progress is to be made up the football ladder.

Bear in mind that dribbling is really close control of the ball, and that without it you cannot slow up a game while your colleagues re-group themselves after being drawn out of position.

One final point: dribbling is a means to an end, not the end itself. Never beat another man just for the sake of doing so. As soon as you have drawn an opponent or created space for a colleague, then let the ball go.

Keep control until the crisis clears!

Brazil's Rivelino beats Franz Beckenbauer of West Germany.

WHEN NOT TO DRIBBLE

Defender B is in trouble, wherever the ball has come from. Three attackers are closing in on him. He *must* bang the ball into touch. He is in trouble if he tries to dribble, and a back pass to the goalkeeper is dangerous.

○ Defenders
● Attackers

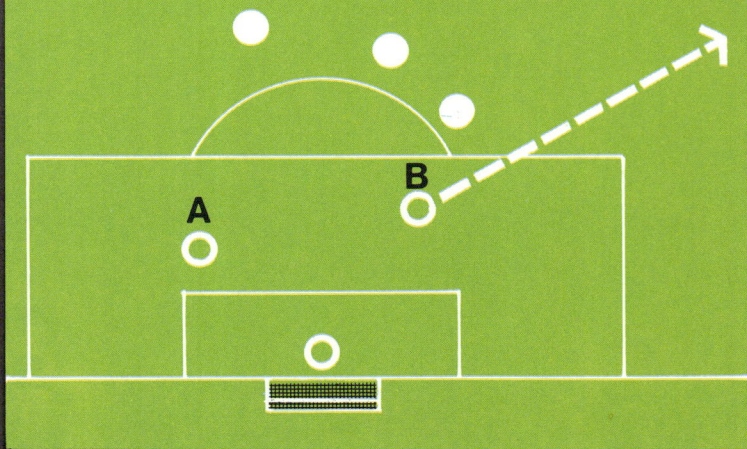

B
A

TEST: Dribbling

Take the ball round the outside of a pitch according to the instructions in the diagram. Have a couple of 'looseners', and then do it against the clock.

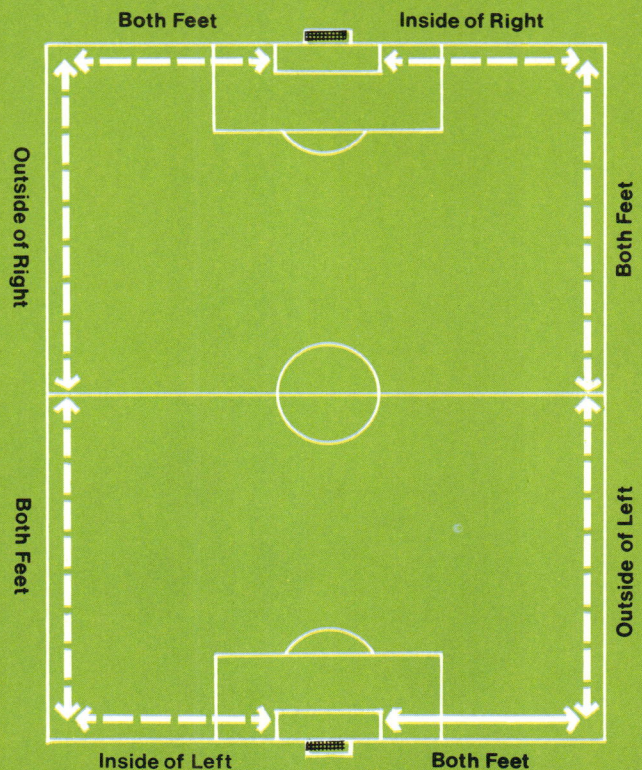

Both Feet   Inside of Right

Outside of Right

Both Feet

Both Feet

Outside of Left

Inside of Left   Both Feet

TEST: Dribbling

Put a polish on your dribbling skill. Place a number of corner flags or other obstacles in a line, and dribble in and out of them. Measure your progress not by how quickly you can do it, but by how many times you need to touch the ball.

Dribbling Brazilian style, with Luisinho in control.

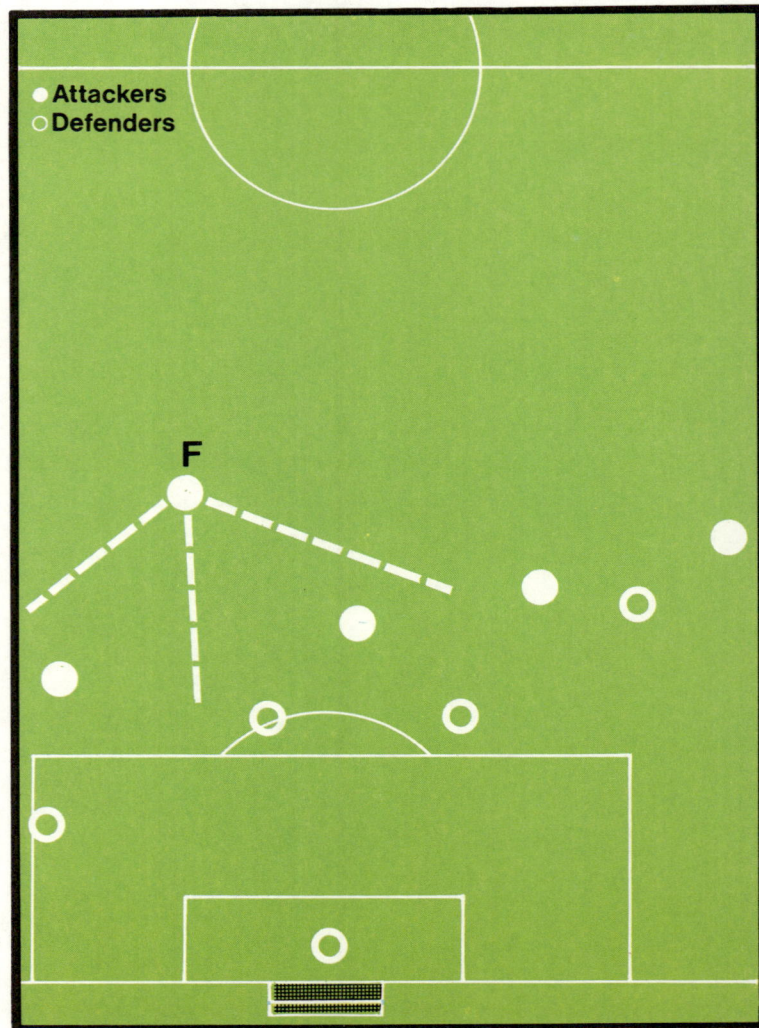

● **Attackers**
○ **Defenders**

F

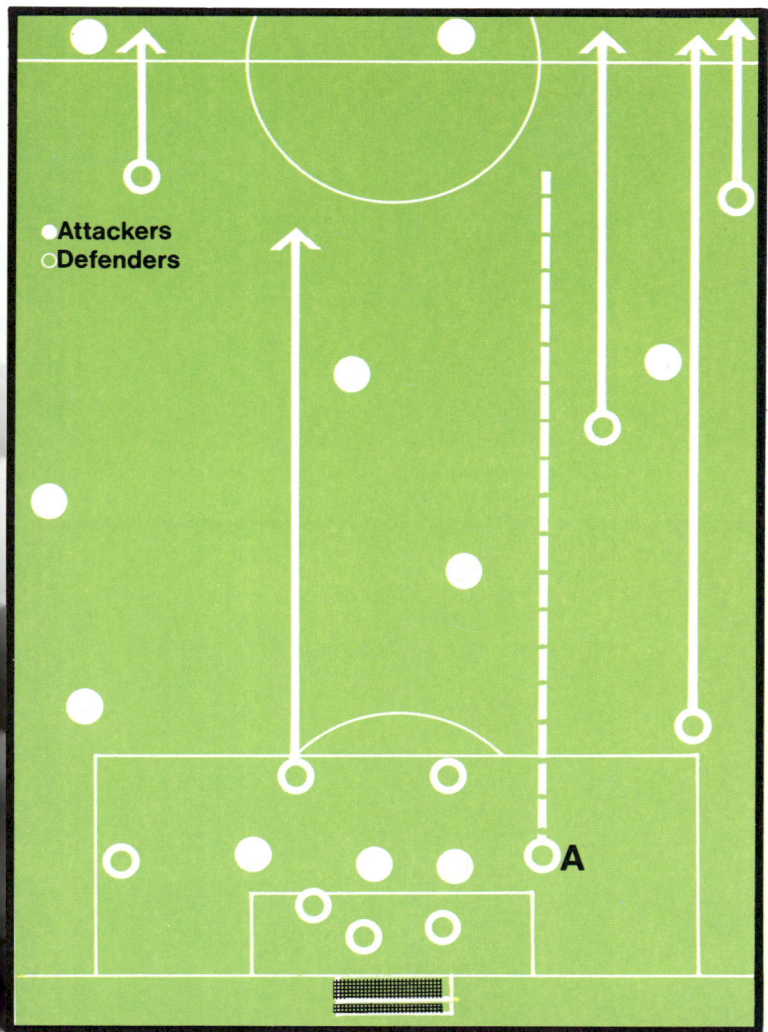

DRIBBLING TACTICS

There are times when you just *have* to dribble, and the diagrams show two such instances. Attacker F, on the left, has four colleagues to whom he could pass, but they are all tightly marked. So he must dribble in any of three directions, until he has drawn one of the opponents out of position. In the right-hand diagram, Defender A must hold the ball (dribble) until such time as his colleagues, all back for a corner, get upfield. If Defender A clears too soon, the ball will come back from one of the two opponents on the half-way line.

Tackling

It might not be entirely true to say that a team is only as good as its hardest tacklers, but it is true to say that the other side are not going to give you the ball. You have to be able to go and get it off them.

Tackling is probably the only purely destructive art in football, but do not imagine that there is no satisfaction in doing it properly and successfully. There is, if only for the reason that not many lads can tackle really well.

This is because the skill demands strength used in the right places, timing and patience. The danger, in a football sense, is that most beginners fling themselves straight into a tackle, instinct ruling reason.

Of course, it is better if you can get the ball from the other side by intercepting it, because that way you have more time to turn the situation to your team's advantage. But if you have to tackle, do it firmly and keep control of the ball. You will need to use it when you come out of the tackle.

A point for team-mates: always try and cover the player who is going into a tackle. If the tackle is not successful, the player making it is probably going to put himself out of the game for the length of time it is going to take him to recover, turn, and get back into position.

Superb tackling by Liverpool's Graeme Souness.

There is more to tackling than just the tackle itself. Positional play, for instance. Defenders should always give themselves a better chance by getting between the attacker and the goal they are defending. It will prevent defenders being beaten by a through pass without the chance of making a tackle.

TEST: Tackling

Place a ball against a wall or post. Move into a tackle, playing the ball as you would if there was a man behind it. If you strike the ball properly, it will remain against the wall. But if the tackle is inaccurate or off balance, the ball will bounce away from the wall.

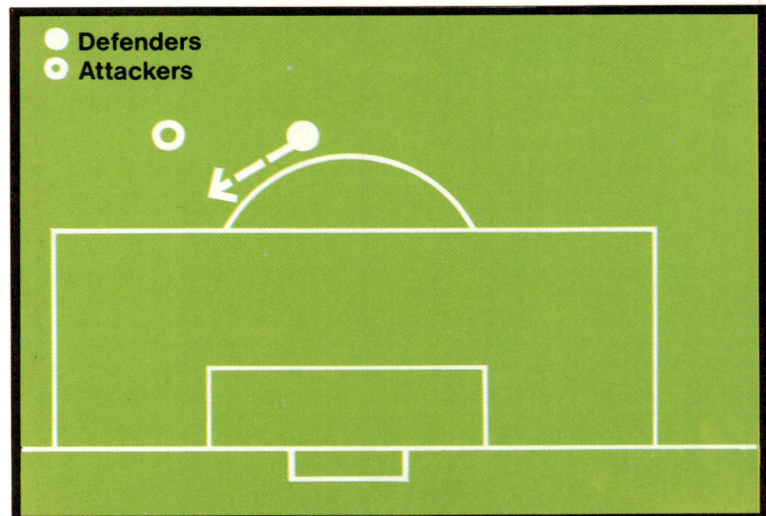

- ● Defenders
- ○ Attackers

BLOCK TACKLE: RIGHT

The player in red is going to win this one. He has his right foot hard up against the ball, and his shoulders and weight are well over the ball.

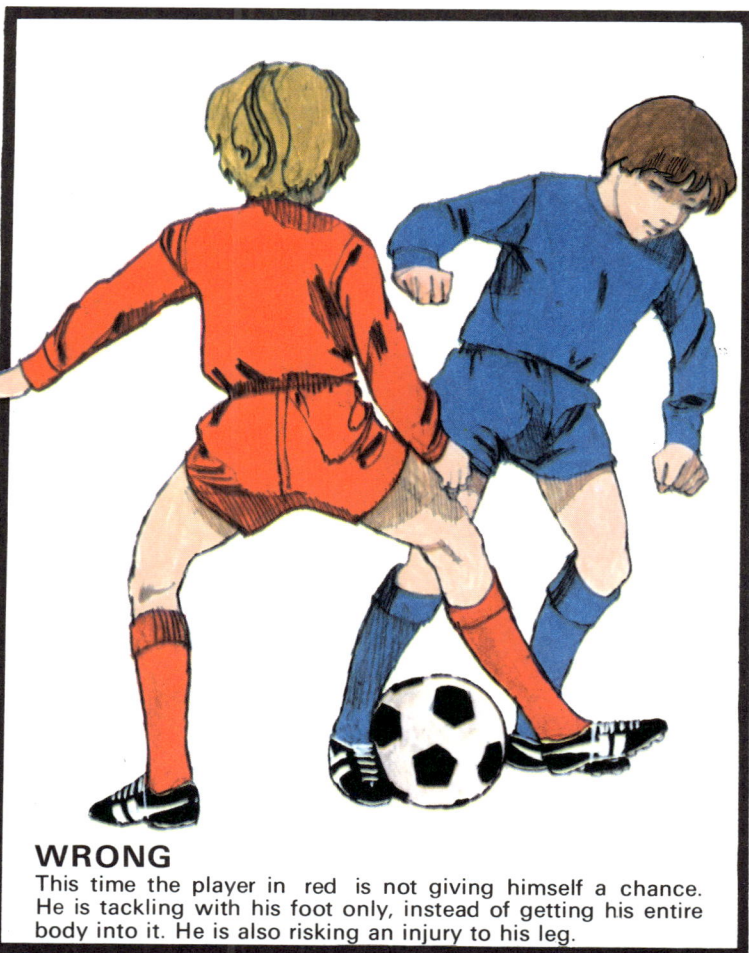

WRONG

This time the player in red is not giving himself a chance. He is tackling with his foot only, instead of getting his entire body into it. He is also risking an injury to his leg.

SLIDING TACKLE

Always tackle with the foot furthest from the ball. It gives you an inch or two of extra length, and lessens the chance of giving away a free-kick for a foul.

Points from the referee

One of the great attractions of Soccer is its sheer simplicity. There is nothing complicated about the game. There are only 17 Laws, and they are so easy to understand that they are the main reason why Soccer has become the game the whole world plays.

You must know these rules like the back of your hand!

If you wish to consult the Laws of the Game, they are to be found in the current edition of the *Referees' Chart and Players' Guide to the Laws of Association Football* produced by the Football Association.

On these two pages we simply outline the main points that the referee will be bearing in mind during the game; they are not the Laws as such. The better you get to know them, the more enjoyment you will get from your game, whether as player or spectator.

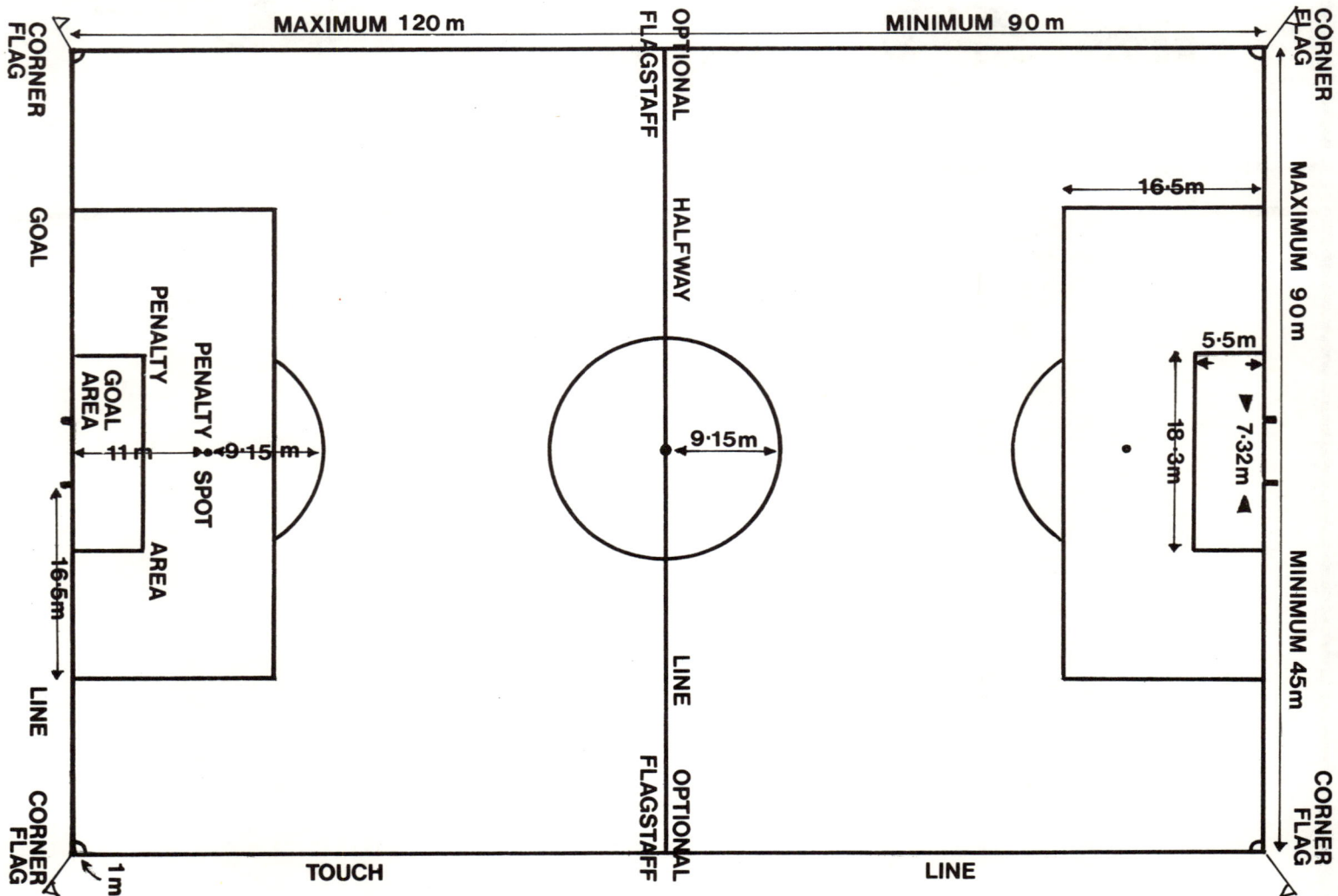

THE FIELD OF PLAY
This is a diagram of the field of play, with the measurements (*reproduced by permission of the Football Association*). Beginners will probably be playing on a rather smaller pitch. The recommended minimum size is 75 metres × 55 metres.

THE BALL
The circumference of the ball should not be more than 71 cm. and not less than 68 cm. At the start of the game it should not weigh more than 453 gm. nor less than 396 gm. Young beginners are advised to use a somewhat smaller ball — size 3 or 4. The ball should not be changed during the game without the referee's permission.

NUMBER OF PLAYERS

A match is played between two teams, each consisting of not more than 11 players, one of whom is the goalkeeper. Substitutes may be used in any match played under the rules of a competition permitting the same. Any of the other players can change places with the goalkeeper, providing the referee has been told.

PLAYERS' EQUIPMENT

A player should not wear anything that is dangerous to another player. Bars and studs on boots must conform to safety standards laid down.

REFEREES

The referee enforces the laws. His decision on points of fact connected with play should be final as far as the result of the game is concerned.

LINESMEN

Two linesmen should be appointed whose duty, subject to the decision of the referee, is to assist the referee to control the game in accordance with the laws.

DURATION OF THE GAME

The duration of the game should be two equal periods of 45 minutes, unless otherwise mutually agreed. Schoolboys' matches are usually 35 or 40 minutes each way.

THE START OF PLAY

The choice of ends and kick-off shall be decided by the toss of a coin. The team winning the toss shall have the option of choice of ends or the kick-off. The referee having signalled, the ball must be kicked from the centre spot into the opposing team's half of the field. Every player shall be in his own half of the field, and every player of the opposing team shall be 9·15 m. from the ball. The player taking the place-kick shall not play the ball a second time, until it has been played by another player. After a goal has been scored, play shall be started in a similar manner by the side which has conceded the goal. At half-time, ends will be changed and the kick-off be taken by a player of the opposite team to that which started the game.

BALL IN AND OUT OF PLAY

The ball is out of play when it has wholly crossed the goal-line or touch-line, and when the game has been stopped by the referee.

METHOD OF SCORING

Except as otherwise provided in the F.A. Laws, a goal is scored when the whole of the ball has passed over the goal-line, between the goalposts and under the cross-bar, providing it has been scored legally and not with hand or arm.

OFF-SIDE

A player is off-side if he is nearer his opponents' goal-line than the ball *at the moment the ball is played* unless: (a) He is in his own half; (b) There are two of his opponents nearer to their own goal-line than he is; (c) The ball last touched an opponent or was played by him; (d) He received the ball direct from a goal-kick, corner-kick, throw-in, or when it was dropped by the referee.

FOULS AND MISCONDUCT

A player committing any of the following offences should have a free-kick awarded against him, or a penalty if the offence has taken place in the penalty area: (a) If he kicks or attempts to kick an opponent; (b) Trips an opponent; (c) Jumps at an opponent; (d) Charges an opponent in a dangerous manner; (e) Charges an opponent from behind (unless the latter is obstructing the player); (f) Strikes or attempts to strike an opponent; (g) Holds an opponent; (h) Pushes an opponent; (i) Handles the ball.

An indirect free-kick, from which a goal cannot be scored, shall be awarded against a player committing any of the following offences: (a) Playing in a dangerous manner; (b) Charging when the ball is not within play distance; (c) Intentionally obstructing an opponent; (d) Charging the goalkeeper, except when he is holding the ball; (e) When playing as goalkeeper the player takes more than four steps whilst holding, bouncing or throwing the ball in the air and catching it again, without releasing it so that it can be played by another player or when he deliberately wastes time.

FREE-KICK

Free-kicks can be classified under two headings: direct, from which a goal can be scored; and indirect, from which a goal cannot be scored. Opposing players shall stand 9·15 m. or more away from the ball when a free-kick is taken. A player cannot score *direct* against his own side from any free-kick.

PENALTY-KICK

A penalty-kick shall be taken from the penalty mark, and all other players except the opposing goalkeeper shall stand outside the penalty area until after the kick is taken. As with a free-kick, the player taking the penalty-kick is not allowed to play the ball again until it has been touched or played by another player.

THROW-IN

When the whole of the ball has passed over the touch-line it must be returned to play by a player from the team opposite to that which last touched it. The thrower should use both hands and deliver the ball from behind and over his head. Part of each foot should be on or behind the line at the moment of delivery. A goal cannot be scored direct from a throw-in.

GOAL-KICK

When the whole of the ball has passed over the goal-line it should be kicked directly back into play from a point within that half of the goal area nearest to where it crossed the line. The ball must be kicked beyond the penalty area before it is in play.

CORNER-KICK

When the whole of the ball passes over the goal-line, excluding that part between the goal-posts, having been last played by a member of the defending side, the ball is returned to play by a member of the attacking side playing it from a corner of the field. The corner flag may not be moved, but a goal can be scored from this kick.

Goalkeeping

A curious fact about goalkeeping and goalkeepers is that usually the young 'keeper has to be pushed into the position – most of us would rather be goal scorers than goal savers. Yet there is no shortage of first-rate goalkeepers in either league or international football! But if you are the smallest fellow in the gang, and ordered into goal because you are not big enough to argue back, here are a few points to remember.

Do not worry if you let a goal in. Admittedly goalkeepers' mistakes are often fatal, but he is usually left stranded by the errors of the players in front of him. It has been estimated that 90 percent of the goals are not the goalkeeper's fault.

Always keep your eye on the ball. It can be very difficult when the ball is down at the other end of the field, but for a goalkeeper concentration is everything. If you can, resist the temptation to chat to people standing behind the goal.

Never forget that although you are nominally the last line of the defence, you are always the first line of the attack as well. When clearing always try to start an attack, and remember that because you are able to use your hands, and so throw the ball, instead of kicking it, you are likely to be more accurate than any of the outfield players. It is an advantage that should never be wasted.

Fine save by Pat Jennings (Spurs and Northern Ireland).

MID-SAVE
Body *behind* the ball: take it deep into the pit of the stomach and wrap hands round the front.

HIGH SAVE
Always make sure that the hands are behind the ball. Otherwise it could slip through, especially in wet weather.

LOW SAVE
As always keep part of the body, in this case knees and legs, *behind* the ball. With legs open, it could go through.

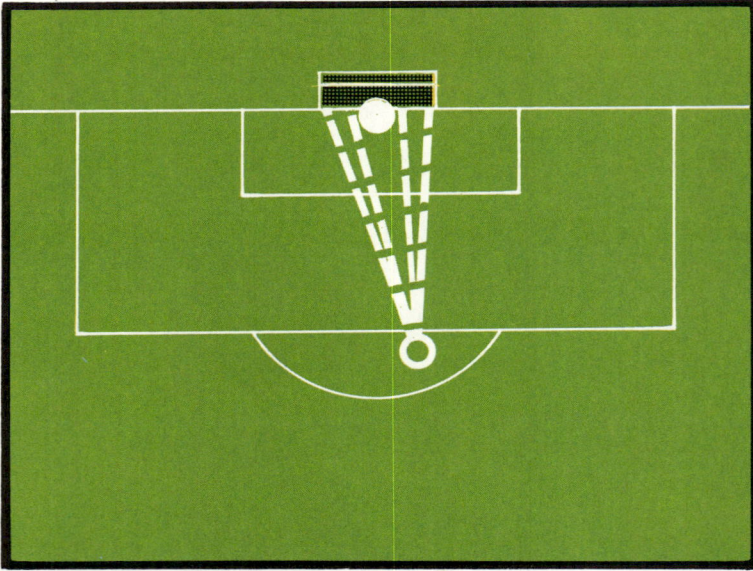

NARROWING ANGLES: WRONG
See the amount of target area a forward has when a goalkeeper stays on his line.

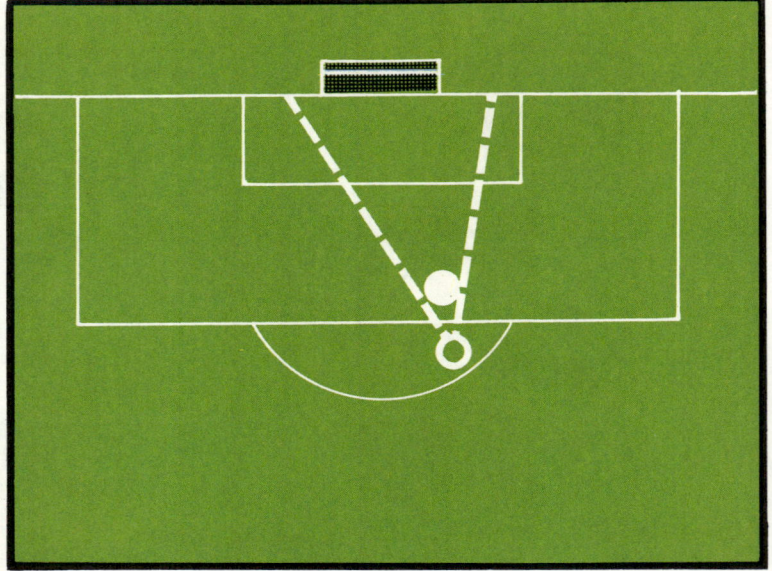

RIGHT
See how the target area is reduced by a good goalkeeper coming forward from his line.

TESTS: Goalkeeping

A goalkeeper who can kick and throw accurately can be worth an extra man to his team. Use the centre circle for practice. Keep kicking and throwing the ball into the circle first bounce, lengthening the distance as you get better.

Practise the rolling test as well. Stand upright with the ball in your hands. Throw it up in the air as high as you can, so that it drops about a metre to your left or right side. While the ball is in the air, do a sideways roll, and as you come out of the roll dive and stop the ball. You should get it before it has bounced three times.

Peter Shilton saves the ball from the English goal.

Defenders

The old football days when one put the biggest, tallest, clumsiest players into the defence and left them to stop the opposition and hammer the ball up the field, have gone for ever. Some of the world's most skilful players are defenders.

To be more concise there are two distinct types of defenders — the flank defenders, who are expected to have sufficient ball control to attack along the wings whenever they have the chance, and the centre-defenders who are the nearest approximation to the old-fashioned centre-halves.

Some of the traditional standards still have to be maintained, however. Defenders must have the ability to tackle. They must develop the knack of getting back into position as soon as possible after an unsuccessful tackle. They must resist the temptation to be enticed out of position. And they must be able to *read* a game so that they always cover their nearest colleague.

Patience is also a virtue. Frequently you are benefitting your side more by jockeying a forward into a certain area of the field, than by risking a tackle too soon which will leave a gap behind you.

SPHERE OF OPERATIONS

Old-fashioned full-backs have now become two of the most important players in any side. They are required to cover the centre defenders and at the same time act as extra attackers down the wings.

THE ANGLE OF TACKLE

Full-back no. 3 is doing a better job than no. 2, who is leaving room for no. 11 to go past him. No. 7 however can only come inside — presumably on his weaker foot.

● Defenders
○ Attackers

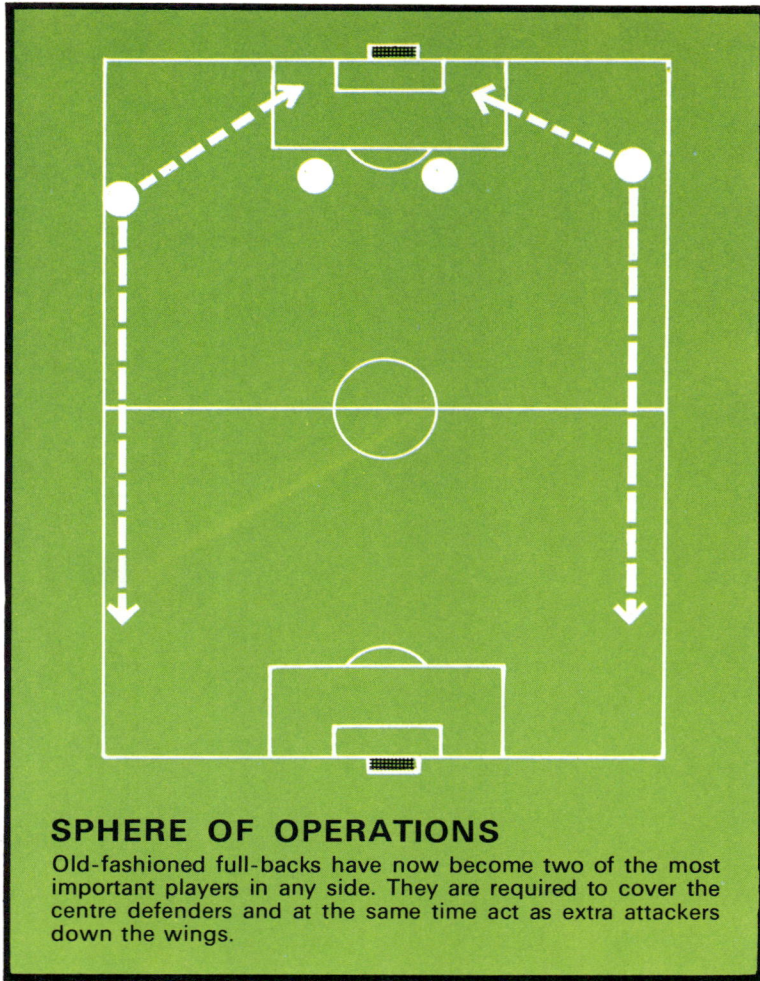

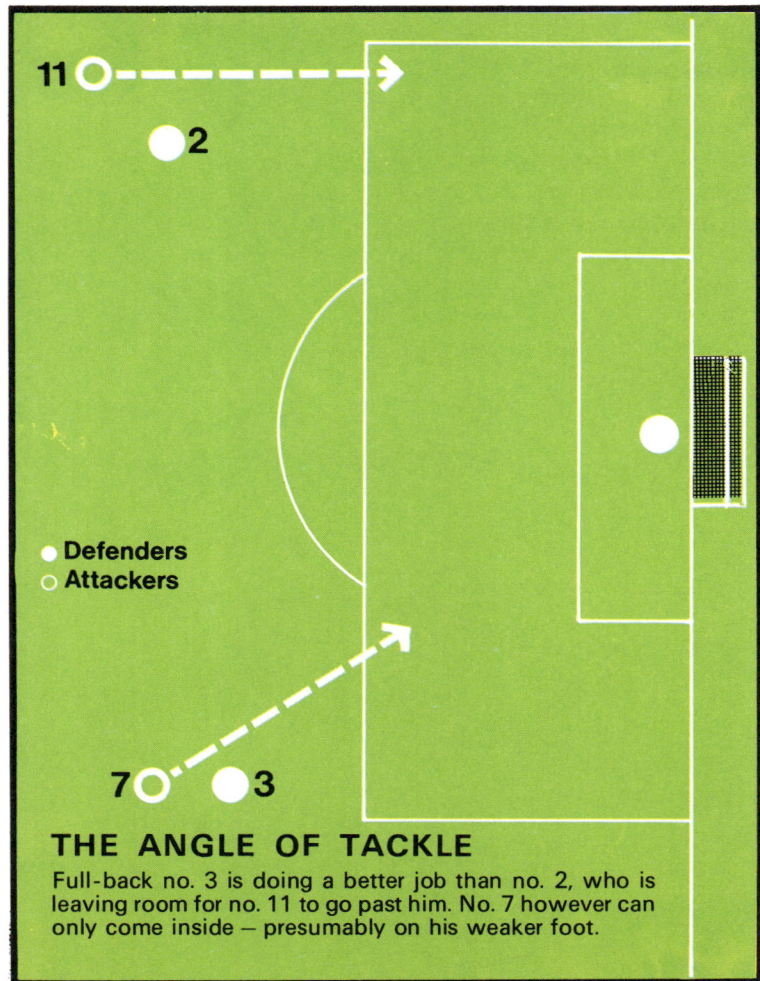

TEST: Defenders

As flank defenders are often called upon to hit balls down the touchline into a narrow 'tunnel', improve your accuracy by putting two corner flags three metres apart, and playing balls through them. Gradually increase your distance from the flags.

31

Kevin Moran of Manchester United defends against Brighton in the 1983 F.A. Cup Final.

Keep position and tackle hard!

Now because the area in which they operate is so vulnerable — right in front of their own goal — centre defenders must develop the ability to clear quickly. That means volleying, for in their sort of situation, there is usually neither time nor inclination for finesse. The best way to improve volleying is to station the two centre backs in their own penalty area, and let the other members of the team loft balls into the goalmouth. The volleyers lose a point each time they let the ball drop to the ground in the goal area, and to increase accuracy they should try and find players with their clearances.

Franz Beckenbauer (West Germany) challenges Brazil.

CENTRE DEFENDERS

Centre defenders, these days, can come in two different guises. There can be a traditional centre-half (No. 5) with a No. 6 or a No. 4 playing with him, as twin centre-halves or centre-backs; or there is the other variant in which the No. 4 or the No. 6 plays slightly behind the No. 5, in the role commonly called 'sweeper'. The sweeper, in effect, plays as a spare man behind the defence, and his role is to see the trouble coming, and do something about it. Should the flank backs be beaten, or the No. 5 miss a tackle, then the sweeper leaps in to the rescue.

Midfield

The midfield players are the team's all-rounders. They bolster the defence, do the donkey-work of fetching and carrying and, when they have half a chance, they should be able to snatch the occasional goal as well.

It is a position which demands the utmost skill in control and passing, and the enthusiasm to do a lot of running off the ball to create diversions for team-mates.

Good midfield men are never out of the game; there are no better examples than the Liverpool pair, Sammy Lee and Graeme Souness.

It has been said that a midfield man needs eyes in the back of his head, and that is hardly an exaggeration. He must be able to anticipate where the goalkeeper can place his clearance, and be running for the 'hole' to make life easy for the 'keeper; he must be able to make accurate passes over 30 metres as well as 13, and also he must be able to remember which of his strikers like the ball at their feet, and which like it wide for them to run on to.

Finally, the midfield man must learn to live with the fact that when he comes off the field after a hard game and his team have won, it is the strikers or the defenders who will probably get the credit.

Stamina plus passing skill!

France's midfield player Platini in action.

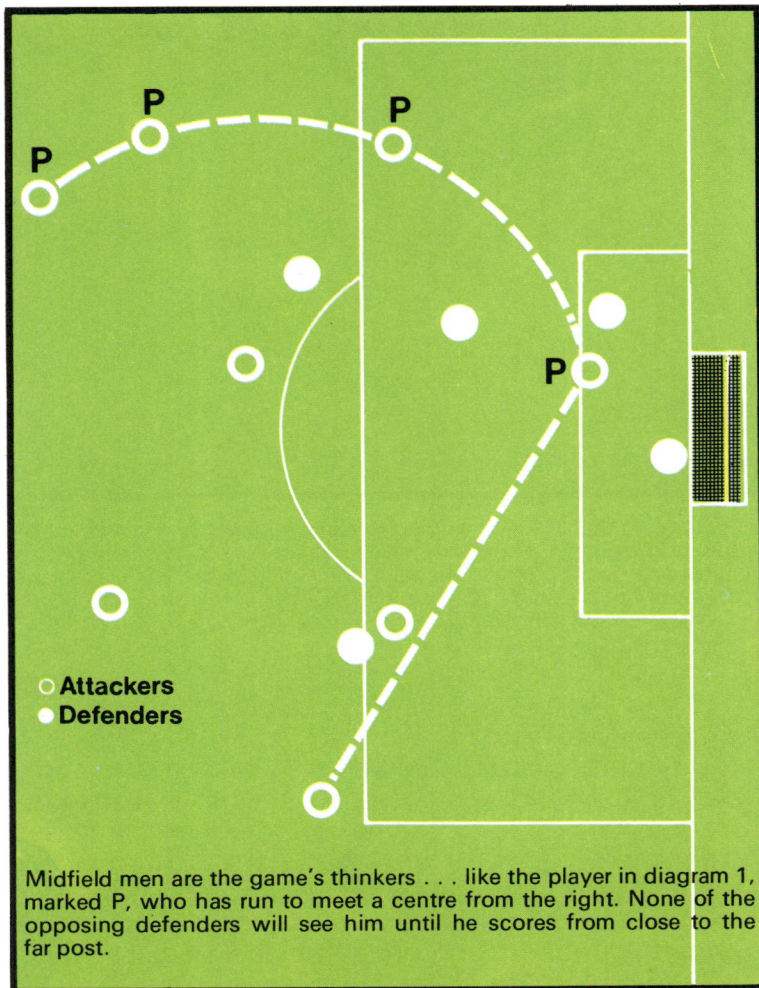

○ Attackers
● Defenders

Midfield men are the game's thinkers . . . like the player in diagram 1, marked P, who has run to meet a centre from the right. None of the opposing defenders will see him until he scores from close to the far post.

Diagram 2 illustrates why midfield men are sometimes called link men. They are the work-horses of the modern football team, joining defence to attack. The entire field is their playing area.

What works like an ox, kicks like a mule, and has eyes in the back of its head?

The midfield player

Bryan Robson showing his midfield form for England against Holland.

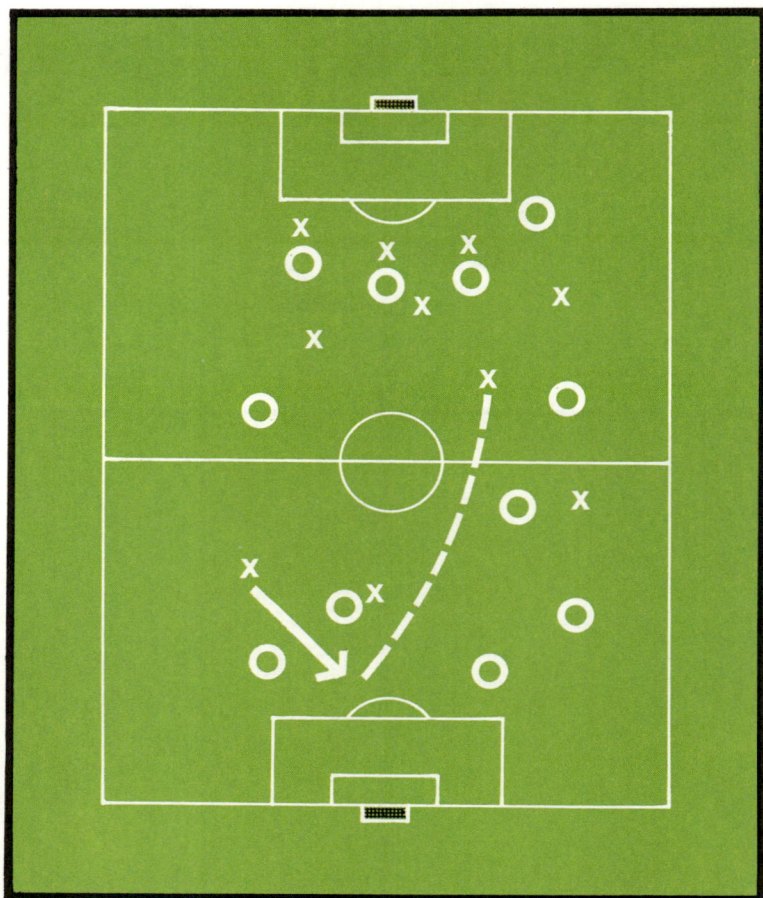

A sure sign that the midfield man is really thinking, is when he makes the long pass out of defence, the quickest way to take a side from defence to attack. In the diagram, the Circles have been attacking. Suddenly a long high ball takes their defence by surprise and the Cross's right striker comes in for a crack at goal.

TEST: Midfield

Midfield men are expected to be able to move the ball quickly and accurately. Get a pal to help you. He plays a ball back to you in the centre circle and from there you lift it into the D at the front of the penalty area. It's not so easy. You are allowed to touch the ball only three times; once to receive it, once to control it, and once to make the pass which must drop into the D first bounce.

Liverpool's Graeme Souness in defensive pose.

Strikers

There is no doubt that strikers are the glamorous players — but, in modern football, they earn it.

The first priority of the position is bravery, for strikers are invariably outnumbered by defenders, and they operate in the most dangerous area, where the boots are flying.

It follows that if strikers are built big and powerful, so much the better. But they cannot afford to be clumsy with the ball as well.

They get such little time in which to work, that they must be able to control and shoot in almost the same instant, and, most important, be able to shoot with either foot.

Heading, too, is all important because frequently the only way in which their team-mates can get the ball into the goalmouth is off a header.

Strikers should also practise and perfect their ability to hold and screen the ball, because there will be a lot of times when they receive it and have to hold it until a colleague can position himself near enough to be able to offer help.

Theirs is the glory. And also the hard work and the bruises.

Steve Coppell shoots for Manchester United despite the efforts of Coventry's Steve Hunt.

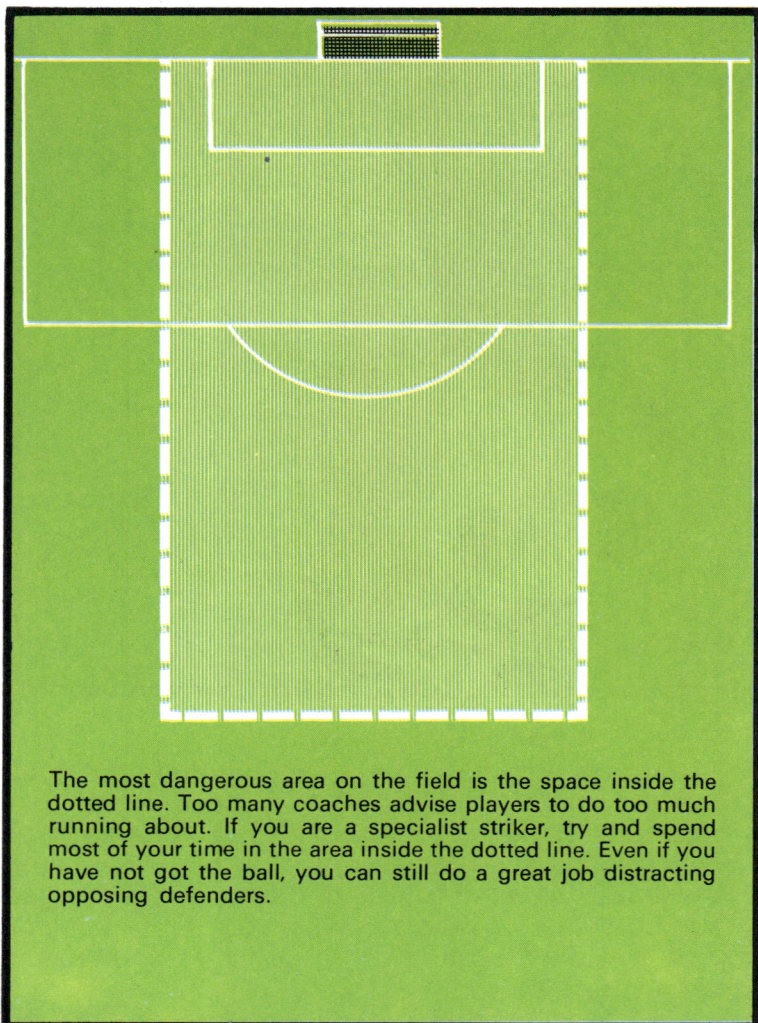

The most dangerous area on the field is the space inside the dotted line. Too many coaches advise players to do too much running about. If you are a specialist striker, try and spend most of your time in the area inside the dotted line. Even if you have not got the ball, you can still do a great job distracting opposing defenders.

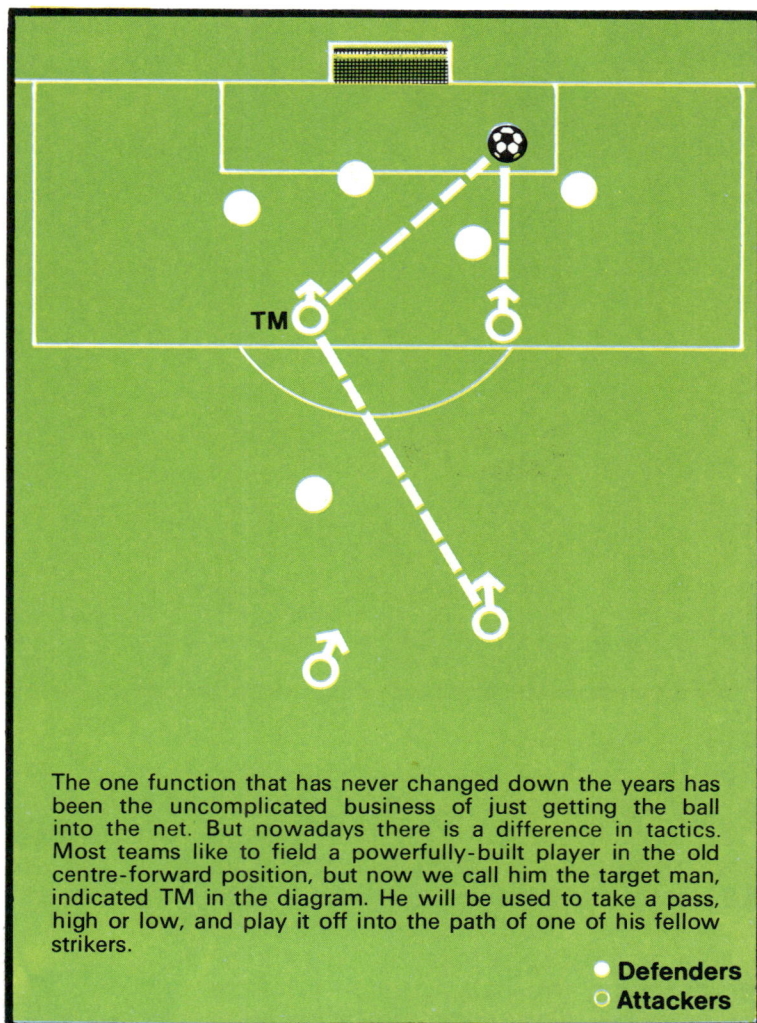

The one function that has never changed down the years has been the uncomplicated business of just getting the ball into the net. But nowadays there is a difference in tactics. Most teams like to field a powerfully-built player in the old centre-forward position, but now we call him the target man, indicated TM in the diagram. He will be used to take a pass, high or low, and play it off into the path of one of his fellow strikers.

● **Defenders**
○ **Attackers**

TEST: Shooting

The best strikers never use more power than they need. The ball only has to go between the posts, it does not have to burst the net as well. So instead of just blasting at the ball indiscriminately, put a couple of corner flags on the goal-line and aim at them. Try and hit the ball quickly and sharply, as if a defender is just coming in to tackle. Get adept at just tucking the ball away. It is not often you will have the whole goal to aim at anyway.

TEST: Heading

There is no better way for any striker to improve his heading ability, a vital part of his technique, than by practising the test shown on p. 12. Another good exercise is to stand on the edge of the penalty area, throw the ball up in the air, and head it into the goal first bounce – *without* moving your feet! Keeping your feet on the ground will improve your timing and your power.

Brazil's striker Zico in their 1982 World Cup match against Argentina.

Speed is the essence!

The shaded area is the best place to put the ball for a striker. Play it closer to the goal and you give the 'keeper a chance to come out and get it. Place it further out, near the edge of the penalty box, and the 'keeper can stay at home. But in the shaded area, he does not know whether to come out or not.

Most 'killer' passes, those that set up goals, can be put into two categories: near-post balls and far-post balls. Most strikers have preferences for one or the other. Big men like the far-post ball, because they can run at it and get most advantage from their height and weight. Smaller strikers like the near-post ball, which takes defenders by surprise. It is a more subtle tactic, and has usually been carefully rehearsed.

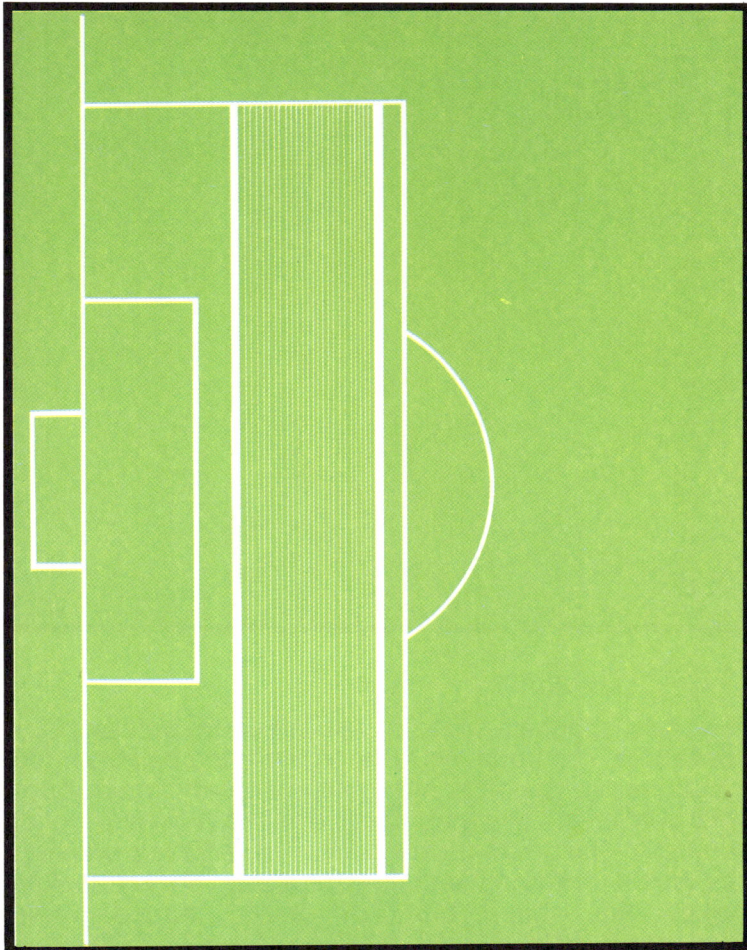

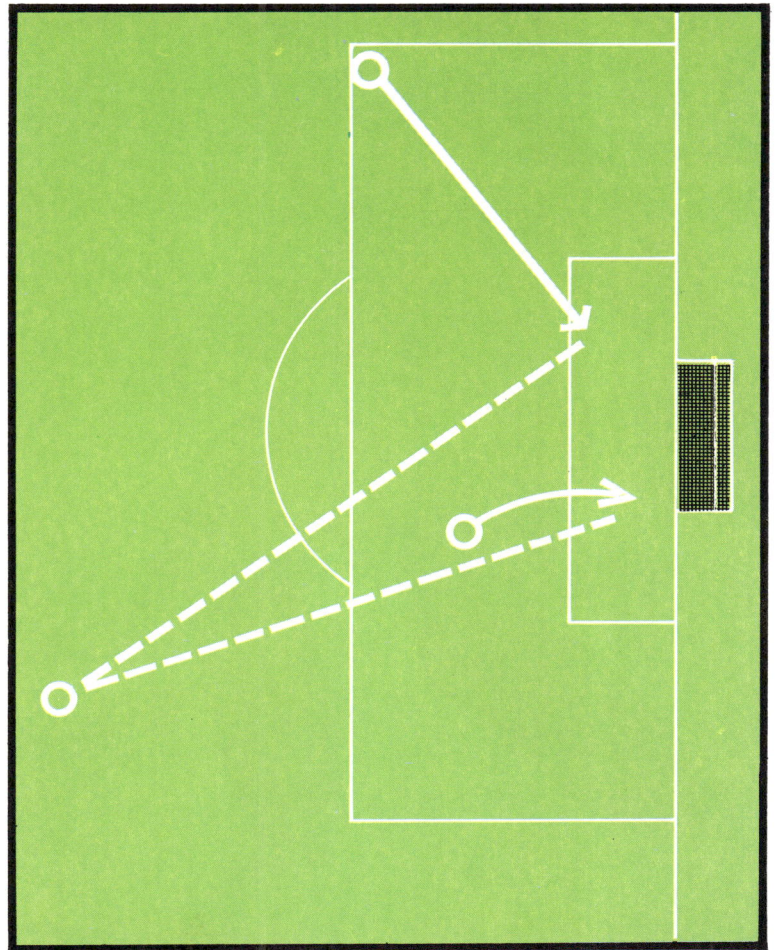

Training alone

Training is a problem, especially for those of you who have to contend with the demands of homework and other activities. The ideal situation, in which the school or youth club team is able to have a couple of training sessions a week with all players present, is so very rarely practicable.

But that is no reason why the player should ignore training completely. There are various modifications of the exercises which we have shown you on preceding pages. All can be adapted for those of you who have to go it alone. Additionally there are the illustrations we present on these pages.

The really important thing is that the exercises are done genuinely. It is far better to work hard for only half an hour, than to take it easy for three times as long.

Do not take training alone too literally. It should not be difficult, surely, to persuade another member of your team to join you. You can then increase the range of your activities, and each of you will spur the other on.

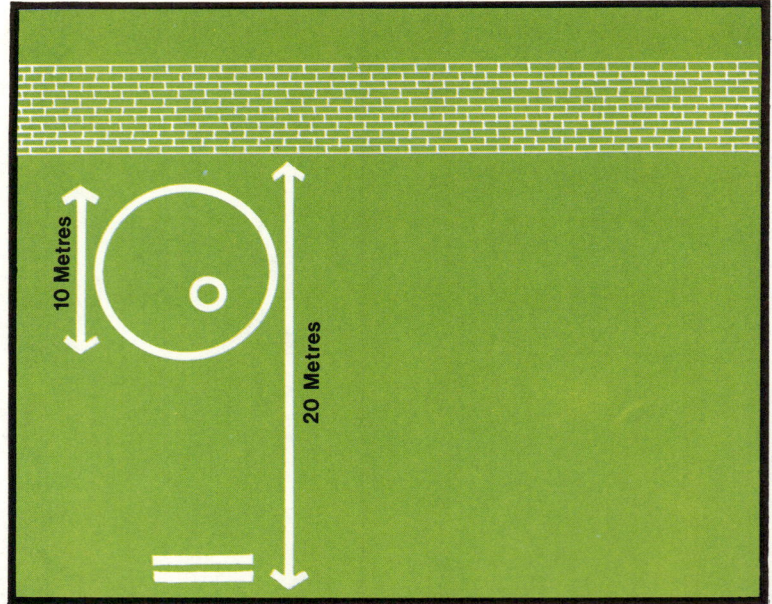

TEST: Control

This exercise will help to polish your control of the ball at speed. Put a ball in the circle. Stand at the edge of the circle nearest to the mark. Run to the mark, turn, and run back to the circle where you play the ball against the wall. Wait for the rebound, control it, and return the ball to the circle. If you have done it properly, of course, you should be standing inside the circle to trap the ball as it comes off the wall. Repeat it again, and again, and again, timing yourself.

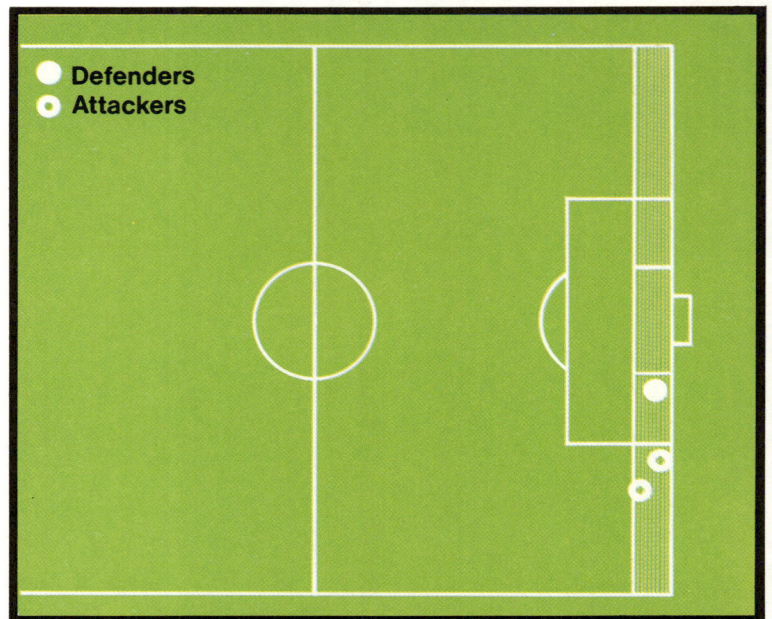

TEST: Defence

The two attackers are to develop their friend's skill as a defender. The attackers have to work the ball from one touchline to the other along an imaginary line through the goal area – in other words down a 5·5-metre wide corridor. The defender learns how to jockey opposition, as well as to time his tackles properly. If the attackers take the ball out of the shaded area, they start again.

TEST: Goalkeeping

Use a wall to give your goalkeeper friend practice. He stands facing the wall. You kick or throw the ball so that he has to save it from the rebound. The goalkeeper faces the wall so that he cannot see which angle the ball is coming off at until the last moment. Then he dives or jumps to save.

The England team in training in 1983.

Milestones of Football History

1848 The first formal rules for the game were drawn up at Cambridge University.

1857 The first football club was formed at Sheffield.

1862 The oldest Football League club, Notts County, came into being.

1863 The Football Association was formed in London on 6 October.

1871 The first F.A. Cup competition was started. Fifteen teams took part: Wanderers (who won), Harrow Chequers, Barnes, Civil Service, Crystal Palace, Upton Park, Hampstead Heathens, Clapham Rovers (all these teams from in or around London), Hitchin, Royal Engineers, Reigate Priory, Maidenhead, Great Marlow (these from the South), Donington Grammar School (from the North) and Queen's Park (from Scotland).

1872 The first international was played at the West of Scotland Cricket Club, Partick, Glasgow. The result: Scotland 0, England 0.

1873 Scottish Football Association formed.

1875 The crossbar replaced tape to define the height of the goal.

1876 Welsh Football Association formed.

1878 Referees used a whistle for the first time.

1880 Irish Football Association formed.

1885 Professionalism was allowed in England.

1888 The Football League was formed. The original 12 members were Accrington, Aston Villa, Blackburn, Bolton, Burnley, Derby, Everton, Notts County, Preston North End (the winners of the first championship), Stoke, West Bromwich Albion and Wolverhampton.

1889 Preston North End became first club to win the F.A. Cup and Football League double.

1891 Nets were used in goals for the first time.

1891 The Scottish League was formed.

1895 The F.A. Cup, held by Aston Villa, was stolen and never recovered.

1897 Aston Villa became the second club to perform the F.A. Cup and Football League double.

1902 25 died in a disaster at Ibrox Park, Glasgow, when the terracing collapsed.

1904 F.I.F.A. (Federation Internationale de Football Association) was formed in Paris.

1905 The first £1,000 transfer took place (Alf Common, from Sunderland to Middlesbrough).

1908 Football was first played in the Olympic Games.

1914 King George V was the first reigning monarch to watch the F.A. Cup Final.

1923 The F.A. Cup Final was held at Wembley for the first time.

1925 The off-side rule was changed so that two defenders instead of three were required between the attacker and the goal when the ball was played.

1926 Huddersfield Town became the first team to win the Football League for three consecutive seasons.

1927 Cardiff City won the F.A. Cup – the only time it has been taken out of England.

1928 The first £10,000 transfer took place (David Jack, from Bolton Wanderers to Arsenal).

1928 Dixie Dean set the record for League goals in a season, with 60 for Everton.

1930 The first World Cup was held in Uruguay. Thirteen nations, mostly from South America, took part and Uruguay won.

1934 Italy won the second World Cup, held in Italy.

1935 Arsenal became the second team to win the League Championship three times in succession.

1936 Joe Payne scored 10 goals for Luton Town against Bristol Rovers, a record in the Football League.

1937 The record British crowd, 149,547, saw Scotland beat England 3–1 at Hampden Park.

1938 Italy retained the World Cup in France.

1946 Thirty-three were killed and hundreds injured

when crush barriers collapsed during a Cup-tie at Burnden Park, Bolton.

1949 A plane crash at Superga, near Turin, killed all on board, including the team of Torino, the Italian champions.

1949 Rangers won the first Scottish treble of League, Cup and League Cup.

1950 Uruguay won the fourth World Cup in Brazil.

1950 Scotland lost at home for the first time to a team from outside the British Isles, Austria winning 1–0 at Hampden Park.

1952 Newcastle United won the F.A. Cup for the second year in succession, the first team to do so in the twentieth century.

1953 England lost at home for the first time to a team from outside the British Isles, Hungary winning 6–3 at Wembley.

1954 West Germany won the fifth World Cup in Switzerland.

1954 U.E.F.A (Union of European Football Associations) was formed.

1955 The European Cup was launched. Real Madrid won the first five competitions.

1958 Eight Manchester United players were killed when the team's plane was involved in a disaster at Munich airport on the way back from a European Cup tie. Eleven others in the party died while several more were badly injured.

1958 Brazil won the sixth World Cup in Sweden.

1961 Tottenham Hotspur became the third team (and the first this century) to perform the F.A. Cup and Football League double.

1962 Brazil retained the World Cup in Chile.

1962 Manchester United became the first British club to pay over £100,000 for a player (Dennis Law from Torino).

1963 In an F.A. Centenary Match, England beat the Rest of the World 2–1.

1964 The worst disaster in soccer history occurred at Lima, Peru, when the crowd rioted during an Olympic Games qualifying match between Peru and Argentina. Three hundred were killed and 500 injured.

1965 Stanley Matthews became the first footballer to be knighted.

1966 England won the eighth World Cup in England.

1966 Substitutes were allowed in the Football League for the first time.

1970 Brazil won the ninth World Cup in Mexico.

1971 On 2 January, 66 people died trying to leave Ibrox Park, Glasgow at the end of the Rangers v Celtic match.

1971 Arsenal achieved the F.A. Cup and Football League double.

1973 Ajax Amsterdam won the European Cup for the third consecutive time.

1974 West Germany won the tenth World Cup in West Germany.

1976 Bayern Munich won the European Cup for the third consecutive time.

1978 Argentina won the eleventh World Cup in Argentina.

1979 The first £1 million transfer took place between British clubs (Trevor Francis from Birmingham City to Nottingham Forest).

1981 Liverpool won the European Cup for the third time.

1981 After 93 seasons the Football League altered its points system, three points being awarded for a win instead of two, to encourage attacking play.

1982 Italy won the World Cup for the third time in Spain.

1982 Diego Maradona became the World's most expensive footballer when joining Barcelona from Boca Juniors for £4 million.

The World Cup

The idea of a World Cup was born at a F.I.F.A. conference in Antwerp in 1920 and the competition came into being in 1930. Uruguay, who had won the Olympic Games title in 1924 and 1928, were chosen as the first hosts and the trophy was named after the president of F.I.F.A., Frenchman Jules Rimet. The competition got off to a discouraging start, as most European nations did not bother to travel to Uruguay for the event, and only 13 countries took part.

The results of the final stages in the 12 competitions to 1982 were as follows (*a.e.t.*: after extra time):

1930 URUGUAY

POOL 1
France 4   Mexico 1
Argentina 1   France 0
Chile 3   Mexico 0
Chile 1   France 0
Argentina 6   Mexico 3
Argentina 3   Chile 1

POOL 2
Yugoslavia 2   Brazil 1
Yugoslavia 4   Bolivia 0
Brazil 4   Bolivia 0

POOL 3
Romania 3   Peru 1
Uruguay 1   Peru 0
Uruguay 4   Romania 0

POOL 4
United States 3   Belgium 0
United States 3   Paraguay 0
Paraguay 1   Belgium 0

SEMI-FINALS
Argentina 6   United States 1
Uruguay 6   Yugoslavia 1

FINAL (Montevideo, 30 July 1930)
Uruguay (1) 4   **Argentina** (2) 2

Leading scorer Stabile (Argentina) 8

1934 ITALY

FIRST ROUND
Italy 7   United States 1
Czechoslovakia 2   Romania 1
Germany 5   Belgium 2
Austria 3   France 2 (*a.e.t.*)
Spain 3   Brazil 1
Switzerland 3   Holland 2
Sweden 3   Argentina 2
Hungary 4   Egypt 2

SECOND ROUND
Germany 2   Sweden 1
Austria 2   Hungary 1
Italy 1   Spain 1 (*a.e.t.*)
Italy 1   Spain 0 (*replay*)
Czechoslovakia 3   Switzerland 2

SEMI-FINALS
Czechoslovakia 3   Germany 1 (in Rome)
Italy 1   Austria 0 (in Milan)

THIRD-PLACE MATCH (Naples)
Germany 3   Austria 2

FINAL (Rome, 10 June 1934)
Italy (0) (1) 2   **Czechoslovakia** (0) (1) 1 (*a.e.t.*)

Leading scorers Schiavio (Italy), Nejedly (Czechoslovakia), Conen (Germany) 4 each

1938 FRANCE

FIRST ROUND
Switzerland 1   Germany 1 (*a.e.t*)
Switzerland 4   Germany 2 (*replay*)
Cuba 3   Romania 3 (*a.e.t.*)
Cuba 2   Romania 1 (*replay*)
Hungary 6   Dutch East Indies 0
France 3   Belgium 1
Czechoslovakia 3   Holland 0 (*a.e.t.*)
Brazil 6   Poland 5 (*a.e.t.*)
Italy 2   Norway 1 (*a.e.t.*)

SECOND ROUND
Sweden 8   Cuba 0
Hungary 2   Switzerland 0
Italy 3   France 1
Brazil 1   Czechoslovakia 1 (*a.e.t.*)
Brazil 2   Czechoslovakia 1 (*replay*)

SEMI-FINALS
Italy 2   Brazil 1 (in Marseilles)
Hungary 5   Sweden 1 (in Paris)

THIRD-PLACE MATCH
(Bordeaux)   Brazil 4   Sweden 2

FINAL (Paris, 19 June 1938)
Italy (3) 4   **Hungary** (1) 2

Leading scorer Leonidas (Brazil) 8

1950 BRAZIL

POOL 1
Brazil 4   Mexico 0
Yugoslavia 3   Switzerland 0
Yugoslavia 4   Mexico 1
Brazil 2   Switzerland 2
Brazil 2   Yugoslavia 0
Switzerland 2   Mexico 1

POOL 2
Spain 3   United States 1
England 2   Chile 0
United States 1   England 0
Spain 2   Chile 0
Spain 1   England 0
Chile 5   United States 2

POOL 3
Sweden 3   Italy 2
Sweden 2   Paraguay 2
Italy 2   Paraguay 0

POOL 4
Uruguay 8   Bolivia 0

FINAL POOL
Final pool replaced knockout system
Uruguay 2   Spain 2
Brazil 7   Sweden 1
Uruguay 3   Sweden 2
Brazil 6   Spain 1
Sweden 3   Spain 1

FINAL (Rio de Janeiro, 16 July 1950)
Uruguay (0) 2   **Brazil** (0) 1
Leading scorer Ademir (Brazil) 7

1954 SWITZERLAND

GROUP 1
Yugoslavia 1   France 0
Brazil 5   Mexico 0
France 3   Mexico 2
Brazil 1   Yugoslavia 1 (*a.e.t.*)

GROUP 2
Hungary 9   South Korea 0
West Germany 4   Turkey 1
Hungary 8   West Germany 3
Turkey 7   South Korea 0
West Germany 7   Turkey 2 (*play-off*)

GROUP 3
Austria 1   Scotland 0
Uruguay 2   Czechoslovakia 0
Austria 5   Czechoslovakia 0
Uruguay 7   Scotland 0

GROUP 4
England 4   Belgium 4 (*a.e.t.*)
Switzerland 2   Italy 1
England 2   Switzerland 0
Italy 4   Belgium 1
Switzerland 4   Italy 1 (*play-off*)

QUARTER-FINALS
West Germany 2   Yugoslavia 0
Hungary 4   Brazil 2
Austria 7   Switzerland 5
Uruguay 4   England 2

SEMI-FINALS
West Germany 6   Austria 1
Hungary 4   Uruguay 2 (*a.e.t.*)

THIRD-PLACE MATCH (Zurich)
Austria 3   Uruguay 1

FINAL (Berne, 4 July 1954)
West Germany (2) 3   **Hungary** (2) 2
Leading scorer Kocsis (Hungary) 11

1958 SWEDEN

GROUP 1
West Germany 3   Argentina 1
Northern Ireland 1   Czechoslovakia 0
West Germany 2   Czechoslovakia 2
Argentina 3   Northern Ireland 1
West Germany 2   Northern Ireland 2
Czechoslovakia 6   Argentina 1
Northern Ireland 2   Czechoslovakia 1 (*a.e.t., play-off*)

GROUP 2
France 7   Paraguay 3
Yugoslavia 1   Scotland 1
Yugoslavia 3   France 2
Paraguay 3   Scotland 2
France 2   Scotland 1
Yugoslavia 3   Paraguay 3

GROUP 3
Sweden 3   Mexico 0
Hungary 1   Wales 1
Wales 1   Mexico 1
Sweden 2   Hungary 1
Hungary 4   Mexico 0
Sweden 0   Wales 0
Wales 2   Hungary 1 (*play-off*)

GROUP 4
England 2   U.S.S.R. 2
Brazil 3   Austria 0
England 0   Brazil 0
U.S.S.R. 2   Austria 0
Brazil 2   U.S.S.R. 0
England 2   Austria 2
U.S.S.R. 1   England 0 (*play-off*)

QUARTER-FINALS
France 4   Northern Ireland 0
West Germany 1   Yugoslavia 0
Sweden 2   U.S.S.R. 0
Brazil 1   Wales 0

SEMI-FINALS
Brazil 5   France 2
Sweden 3   West Germany 1

THIRD-PLACE MATCH
(Gothenburg)
France 6   West Germany 3

FINAL (Stockholm, 29 June 1958)
Brazil (2) 5   **Sweden** (1) 2

Leading scorer Fontaine (France) 13

1962 CHILE

GROUP 1
Uruguay 2   Columbia 1
U.S.S.R. 2   Yugoslavia 0
Yugoslavia 3   Uruguay 1
U.S.S.R. 4   Columbia 4
U.S.S.R. 2   Uruguay 1
Yugoslavia 5   Columbia 0

GROUP 2
Chile 3   Switzerland 1
West Germany 0   Italy 0
Chile 2   Italy 0
West Germany 2   Switzerland 1
West Germany 2   Chile 0
Italy 3   Switzerland 0

GROUP 3
Brazil 2   Mexico 0
Czechoslovakia 1   Spain 0
Brazil 0   Czechoslovakia 0
Spain 1   Mexico 0
Brazil 2   Spain 1
Mexico 3   Czechoslovakia 1

GROUP 4
Argentina 1   Bulgaria 0
Hungary 2   England 1
England 3   Argentina 1
Hungary 6   Bulgaria 1
Argentina 0   Hungary 0
England 0   Bulgaria 0

QUARTER-FINALS
Yugoslavia 1   West Germany 0
Brazil 3   England 1
Chile 2   U.S.S.R. 1
Czechoslovakia 1   Hungary 0

SEMI-FINALS
Brazil 4   Chile 2
Czechoslovakia 3   Yugoslavia 1

THIRD-PLACE MATCH
(Santiago)
Chile 1   Yugoslavia 0

FINAL (Santiago, 17 June 1962)

Brazil (1) 3 **Czechoslovakia** (1) 1

1966 ENGLAND

GROUP 1
England 0   Uruguay 0
France 1   Mexico 1
Uruguay 2   France 1
England 2   Mexico 0
Uruguay 0   Mexico 0
England 2   France 0

GROUP 2
West Germany 5   Switzerland 0
Argentina 2   Spain 1
Spain 2   Switzerland 1
Argentina 0   West Germany 0
Argentina 2   Switzerland 0
West Germany 2   Spain 1

GROUP 3
Brazil 2   Bulgaria 0
Portugal 3   Hungary 1
Hungary 3   Brazil 1
Portugal 3   Bulgaria 0
Portugal 3   Brazil 1
Hungary 3   Bulgaria 1

GROUP 4
U.S.S.R. 3   North Korea 0
Italy 2   Chile 0
Chile 1   North Korea 1
U.S.S.R. 1   Italy 0
North Korea 1   Italy 0
U.S.S.R. 2   Chile 1

QUARTER-FINALS
England 1   Argentina 0
West Germany 4   Uruguay 0
Portugal 5   North Korea 3
U.S.S.R. 2   Hungary 1

SEMI-FINALS
West Germany 2   U.S.S.R. 1
England 2   Portugal 1

THIRD-PLACE MATCH
(Wembley)
Portugal 2   U.S.S.R. 1

FINAL (Wembley, 30 July 1966)
England (1) (2) **4   West Germany** (1) (2) 2 (a.e.t.)

Leading scorer Eusebio (Portugal) 9

1970 MEXICO

GROUP A
Mexico 0   U.S.S.R. 0
Belgium 3   El Salvador 0
U.S.S.R. 4   Belgium 1
Mexico 4   El Salvador 0
U.S.S.R. 2   El Salvador 0
Mexico 1   Belgium 0

GROUP B
Uruguay 2   Israel 0
Italy 1   Sweden 0
Uruguay 0   Italy 0
Israel 1   Sweden 1
Sweden 1   Uruguay 0
Israel 0   Italy 0

GROUP C
England 1   Romania 0
Brazil 4   Czechoslovakia 1
Romania 2   Czechoslovakia 1
Brazil 1   England 0
Brazil 3   Romania 2
England 1   Czechoslovakia 0

GROUP D
Peru 3   Bulgaria 2
West Germany 2   Morocco 1

Peru 3   Morocco 0
West Germany 5   Bulgaria 2
West Germany 3   Peru 1
Bulgaria 1   Morocco 1

QUARTER-FINALS
Uruguay 1   U.S.S.R. 0 (a.e.t.)
Italy 4   Mexico 1
Brazil 4   Peru 2
West Germany 3   England 2 (a.e.t.)

SEMI-FINALS
Italy 4   West Germany 3 (a.e.t.)
Brazil 3   Uruguay 1

THIRD-PLACE MATCH
(Mexico City)
West Germany 1   Uruguay 0

FINAL (Mexico City, 21 June 1970)
Brazil (1) **4   Italy** (1) 1

Leading scorer Muller (West Germany) 10

1974 WEST GERMANY

GROUP 1
West Germany 1   Chile 0
East Germany 2   Australia 0
West Germany 3   Australia 0
East Germany 1   Chile 1
Chile 0   Australia 0
East Germany 1   West Germany 0

GROUP 2
Brazil 0   Yugoslavia 0
Scotland 2   Zaire 0
Brazil 0   Scotland 0
Yugoslavia 9   Zaire 0
Scotland 1   Yugoslavia 1
Brazil 3   Zaire 0

GROUP 3
Holland 2   Uruguay 0
Sweden 0   Bulgaria 0
Holland 0   Sweden 0
Bulgaria 1   Uruguay 1
Holland 4   Bulgaria 1
Sweden 3   Uruguay 0

GROUP 4
Italy 3   Haiti 1
Poland 3   Argentina 2
Argentina 1   Italy 1
Poland 7   Haiti 0
Argentina 4   Haiti 1
Poland 2   Italy 1

GROUP A
Brazil 1   East Germany 0
Holland 4   Argentina 0
Holland 2   East Germany 0
Brazil 2   Argentina 1
Holland 2   Brazil 0
Argentina 1   East Germany 1

GROUP B
Poland 1   Sweden 0
West Germany 2   Yugoslavia 0
Poland 2   Yugoslavia 1
West Germany 4   Sweden 2
Sweden 2   Yugoslavia 1
West Germany 1   Poland 0

THIRD-PLACE MATCH
(Munich)
Poland 1   Brazil 0

FINAL (Munich, 7 July 1974)
West Germany 2   Holland 1

Leading scorer Lato (Poland) 7

1978 ARGENTINA

GROUP 1
Italy 2   France 1
Argentina 2   Hungary 1
Italy 3   Hungary 1
Argentina 2   France 1
France 3   Hungary 1
Italy 1   Argentina 0

GROUP 2
West Germany 0   Poland 0
Tunisia 3   Mexico 1
Poland 1   Tunisia 0
West Germany 6   Mexico 0
Poland 3   Mexico 1
West Germany 0   Tunisia 0

GROUP 3
Austria 2   Spain 1
Brazil 1   Sweden 1
Austria 1   Sweden 0
Brazil 0   Spain 0
Spain 1   Sweden 0
Brazil 1   Austria 0

GROUP 4
Peru 3   Scotland 1
Holland 3   Iran 0
Scotland 1   Iran 1
Holland 0   Peru 0
Peru 4   Iran 1
Scotland 3   Holland 2

GROUP A
West Germany 0   Italy 0
Holland 5   Austria 1
Italy 1   Austria 0
Holland 2   West Germany 2
Holland 2   Italy 1
Austria 3   West Germany 2

GROUP B
Brazil 3   Peru 0
Argentina 2   Poland 0
Poland 1   Peru 0
Argentina 0   Brazil 0
Brazil 3   Poland 1
Argentina 6   Peru 0

THIRD-PLACE MATCH
(Buenos Aires)
Brazil 2   Italy 1

FINAL (Buenos Aires, 25 June 1978)
Argentina 3   **Holland** 1 (a.e.t.)

Leading scorer Kempes (Argentina) 6

1982 SPAIN

GROUP 1
Italy 0   Poland 0
Peru 0   Cameroon 0
Italy 1   Peru 1
Poland 0   Cameroon 0
Poland 5   Peru 1
Italy 1   Cameroon 1

GROUP 2
Algeria 2   West Germany 1
Austria 1   Chile 0
West Germany 4   Chile 1
Austria 2   Algeria 0
Algeria 3   Chile 2
West Germany 1   Austria 0

GROUP 3
Belgium 1   Argentina 0
Hungary 10   El Salvador 1
Argentina 4   Hungary 1
Belgium 1   El Salvador 0
Belgium 1   Hungary 1
Argentina 2   El Salvador 0

GROUP 4
England 3   France 1
Czechoslovakia 1   Kuwait 1
England 2   Czechoslovakia 0
France 4   Kuwait 1
France 1   Czechoslovakia 1
England 1   Kuwait 0

GROUP 5
Spain 1   Honduras 1
Northern Ireland 0   Yugoslavia 0
Spain 2   Yugoslavia 1
Honduras 1   Northern Ireland 1
Yugoslavia 1   Honduras 0
Northern Ireland 1   Spain 0

GROUP 6
Brazil 2   U.S.S.R. 1
Scotland 5   New Zealand 2
Brazil 4   Scotland 1
U.S.S.R. 3   New Zealand 0
Scotland 2   U.S.S.R. 2
Brazil 4   New Zealand 0

GROUP A
Poland 3   Belgium 0
U.S.S.R. 1   Belgium 0
Poland 0   U.S.S.R. 0

GROUP B
West Germany 0   England 0
West Germany 2   Spain 1
Spain 0   England 0

GROUP C
Italy 2   Argentina 1
Brazil 3   Argentina 1
Italy 3   Brazil 2

GROUP D
France 1   Austria 0
Northern Ireland 2   Austria 2
France 4   Northern Ireland 1

SEMI-FINALS
Italy 2   Poland 0
West Germany 3   France 3
(West Germany won on penalties 5–4)

THIRD-PLACE MATCH
(Alicante)   Poland 3   France 2

FINAL (Madrid, 11 July 1982)
Italy (0) 3   **West Germany** (0) 1

Leading scorer Rossi (Italy) 6

Overall Top Scorers in World Cup Final Stages

Muller (West Germany)	14	Rossi (Italy)	9
Fontaine (France)	13	Vava (Brazil)	9
Pelé (Brazil)	12	Leonidas (Brazil)	8
Kocsis (Hungary)	11	Morlock (West Germany)	8
Rahn (West Germany)	10	Rummenigge (West Germany)	8
Lato (Poland)	10	Schiaffino (Uruguay)	8
Seeler (West Germany)	10	Stabile (Argentina)	8
Ademir (Brazil)	9	Rep (Holland)	7
Cubillas (Peru)	9	Tichy (Hungary)	7
Eusebio (Portugal)	9	Zsengeller (Hungary)	7
Jairzinho (Brazil)	9		

The Football League Championship

1888–89	Preston North End	1924–25	Huddersfield T.	1963–64	Liverpool
1889–90	Preston North End	1925–26	Huddersfield T.	1964–65	Manchester U.
1890–91	Everton	1926–27	Newcastle U.	1965–66	Liverpool
1891–92	Sunderland	1927–28	Everton	1966–67	Manchester U.
1892–93	Sunderland	1928–29	Sheffield W.	1967–68	Manchester C.
1893–94	Aston Villa	1929–30	Sheffield W.	1968–69	Leeds U.
1894–95	Sunderland	1930–31	Arsenal	1969–70	Everton
1895–96	Aston Villa	1931–32	Everton	1970–71	Arsenal
1896–97	Aston Villa	1932–33	Arsenal	1971–72	Derby Co.
1897–98	Sheffield U.	1933–34	Arsenal	1972–73	Liverpool
1898–99	Aston Villa	1934–35	Arsenal	1973–74	Leeds U.
1899–1900	Aston Villa	1935–36	Sunderland	1974–75	Derby Co.
1900–01	Liverpool	1936–37	Manchester C.	1975–76	Liverpool
1901–02	Sunderland	1937–38	Arsenal	1976–77	Liverpool
1902–03	The Wednesday	1938–39	Everton	1977–78	Nottingham F.
1903–04	The Wednesday	1946–47	Liverpool	1978–79	Liverpool
1904–05	Newcastle U.	1947–48	Arsenal	1979–80	Liverpool
1905–06	Liverpool	1948–49	Portsmouth	1980–81	Aston Villa
1906–07	Newcastle U.	1949–50	Portsmouth	1981–82	Liverpool
1907–08	Manchester U.	1950–51	Tottenham H.	1982–83	Liverpool
1908–09	Newcastle U.	1951–52	Manchester U.	1983–84	Liverpool
1909–10	Aston Villa	1952–53	Arsenal		
1910–11	Manchester U.	1953–54	Wolverhampton W.		
1911–12	Blackburn R.	1954–55	Chelsea		
1912–13	Sunderland	1955–56	Manchester U.		
1913–14	Blackburn R.	1956–57	Manchester U.		
1914–15	Everton	1957–58	Wolverhampton W.		
1919–20	W.B.A	1958–59	Wolverhampton W.		
1920–21	Burnley	1959–60	Burnley		
1921–22	Liverpool	1960–61	Tottenham H.		
1922–23	Liverpool	1961–62	Ipswich T.		
1923–24	Huddersfield T.	1962–63	Everton		

TOTALS

With seven Championships in nine years between 1975–76 and 1983–84 Liverpool have taken a big lead in total Championships won. This is the breakdown:

Liverpool	15
Arsenal	8
Manchester U.	7
Everton	7
Aston Villa	7

Sunderland	6	Portsmouth	2	Derby Co.	2
Newcastle U.	4	Preston N. E.	2	Chelsea	1
Sheffield W.	4	Burnley	2	Sheffield U.	1
Huddersfield T.	3	Manchester C.	2	W.B.A.	1
Wolverhampton W.	3	Tottenham H.	2	Ipswich T.	1
Blackburn R.	2	Leeds U.	2	Nottingham F.	1

Scottish League Champions

1890–91	Dumbarton/ Rangers	1914–15	Celtic	1933–34	Rangers	1959–60	Hearts
1891–92	Dumbarton	1915–16	Celtic	1934–35	Rangers	1960–61	Rangers
1892–93	Celtic	1916–17	Celtic	1935–36	Celtic	1961–62	Dundee
1893–94	Celtic	1917–18	Rangers	1936–37	Rangers	1962–63	Rangers
1894–95	Hearts	1918–19	Celtic	1937–38	Celtic	1963–64	Rangers
1895–96	Celtic	1919–20	Rangers	1938–39	Rangers	1964–65	Kilmarnock
1896–97	Hearts	1920–21	Rangers	1946–47	Rangers	1965–66	Celtic
1897–98	Celtic	1921–22	Celtic	1947–48	Hibernian	1966–67	Celtic
1898–99	Rangers	1922–23	Rangers	1948–49	Rangers	1967–68	Celtic
1899–1900	Rangers	1923–24	Rangers	1949–50	Rangers	1968–69	Celtic
1900–01	Rangers	1924–25	Rangers	1950–51	Hibernian	1969–70	Celtic
1901–02	Rangers	1925–26	Celtic	1951–52	Hibernian	1970–71	Celtic
1902–03	Hibernian	1926–27	Rangers	1952–53	Rangers	1971–72	Celtic
1903–04	Third Lanark	1927–28	Rangers	1953–54	Celtic	1972–73	Celtic
1904–05	Celtic	1928–29	Rangers	1954–55	Aberdeen	1973–74	Celtic
1905–06	Celtic	1929–30	Rangers	1955–56	Rangers	1974–75	Rangers
1906–07	Celtic	1930–31	Rangers	1956–57	Rangers	1975–76	Rangers
1907–08	Celtic	1931–32	Motherwell	1957–58	Hearts	1976–77	Celtic
1908–09	Celtic	1932–33	Rangers	1958–59	Rangers	1977–78	Rangers
1909–10	Celtic					1978–79	Celtic
1910–11	Rangers					1979–80	Aberdeen
1911–12	Rangers					1980–81	Celtic
1912–13	Rangers					1981–82	Celtic
1913–14	Celtic					1982–83	Dundee U.
						1983–84	Aberdeen

TOTALS
Rangers and Celtic have won 69 of 87 Scottish Championships and shared another. Full totals are: Rangers 36 + 1 shared, Celtic 33, Hearts 4, Hibernian 4, Aberdeen 3, Dumbarton 1 + 1 shared, Third Lanark 1, Motherwell 1, Dundee 1, Kilmarnock 1, Dundee United 1.

The European Competitions

The first competition to involve clubs from many European countries was the European Cup, the brainchild of Gabriel Hanot, football editor of the French newspaper *L'Equipe*. When the English club, Wolverhampton Wanderers, beat the Hungarian club, Honved, in December 1954, some English newspapers claimed Wolves were 'Champions of Europe'. Hanot proposed a tournament to discover the real champions of Europe; his plans were approved by F.I.F.A., and U.E.F.A. organized the first European Cup in 1956, or to give it the name engraved upon it, the 'Coupe des Clubs Champions Europeens'. To win it, League champions of each country compete with each other on a knock-out basis.

The competition was a success, and in time others followed. In 1961 came the European Cup Winners Cup, for which each country's cup winners competed.

Meanwhile, in 1955 an International Inter-City Industrial Fairs Cup had been started, between European cities (rather than clubs) which held trade fairs – thus in the first tournament a team representing London took part. The first competition ran from 1955 to 1958, but soon settled down to an annual tournament between 'normal' clubs. In 1966 it became the European Fairs Cup, and in 1971 the U.E.F.A. Cup. It is contested by leading clubs from each country failing to qualify for either the European Cup or the European Cup Winners Cup.

Inter v. Lanerossi Vicenza – a header off Mazzola.

EUROPEAN CUP FINALS

1956	Real Madrid beat Stade de Reims (4–3) in Paris
1957	Real Madrid beat AC Fiorentina (2–0) in Madrid
1958	Real Madrid beat AC Milan (3–2, *a.e.t.*) in Brussels
1959	Real Madrid beat Stade de Reims (2–0) in Stuttgart
1960	Real Madrid beat Eintracht Frankfurt (7–3) in Glasgow
1961	Benfica beat Barcelona (3–2) in Berne
1962	Benfica beat Real Madrid (5–3) in Amsterdam
1963	A.C. Milan beat Benfica (2–1) in London
1964	Inter-Milan beat Real Madrid (3–1) in Vienna
1965	Inter Milan beat Benfica (1–0) in Milan
1966	Real Madrid beat Partizan Belgrade (2–1) in Brussels
1967	Celtic beat Inter-Milan (2–1) in Lisbon
1968	Manchester U. beat Benfica (4–1, *a.e.t.*) in London
1969	A.C. Milan beat Ajax Amsterdam (4–1) in Madrid
1970	Feyenoord beat Celtic (2–1, *a.e.t.*) in Milan
1971	Ajax Amsterdam beat Panathinaikos (2–0) in London
1972	Ajax Amsterdam beat Inter-Milan (2–0) in Rotterdam
1973	Ajax Amsterdam beat Juventus (1–0) in Belgrade
1974	Bayern Munich beat Atletico Madrid (After 1–1 draw in Brussels) (4–0) in Brussels
1975	Bayern Munich beat Leeds U. (2–0) in Paris
1976	Bayern Munich beat St Etienne (1–0) in Glasgow
1977	Liverpool beat Borussia Moenchengladbach (3–1) in Rome
1978	Liverpool beat F.C. Bruges (1–0) in London
1979	Nottingham Forest beat Malmo (1–0) in Munich
1980	Nottingham Forest beat S.V. Hamburg (1–0) in Madrid
1981	Liverpool beat Real Madrid (1–0) in Paris
1982	Aston Villa beat Bayern Munich (1–0) in Rotterdam
1983	S.V. Hamburg beat Juventus (1–0) in Athens
1984	Liverpool beat Roma (1–1, 4-2 on penalties *a.e.t*) in Rome

EUROPEAN CUP WINNERS CUP FINALS

1961	A.C. Fiorentina beat Rangers (4–1) aggregate score
1962	Atletico Madrid beat F.C. Fiorentina (3–0) in Stuttgart
1963	Tottenham H. beat Atletico Madrid (5–1) in Rotterdam
1964	Sporting Club Lisbon beat M.T.K. Budapest (After 3–3 draw in Brussels) (1–0) in Antwerp
1965	West Ham U. beat T.S.V. Munich 1860 (2–0) in London
1966	Borussia Dortmund beat Liverpool (2–1, a.e.t.) in Glasgow
1967	Bayern Munich beat Rangers (1–0, a.e.t.) in Nuremberg
1968	A.C. Milan beat S.V. Hamburg (2–0) in Rotterdam
1969	Slovan Bratislava beat Barcelona (3–2) in Basle
1970	Manchester City beat Gornik Zabrze (2–1) in Vienna
1971	Chelsea beat Real Madrid (After 1–1 draw in Athens) (2–1) in Athens
1972	Rangers beat Dynamo Moscow (3–2) in Barcelona
1973	A.C. Milan beat Leeds U. (1–0) in Salonika
1974	F.C. Magdeburg beat A.C. Milan (2–0) in Rotterdam
1975	Dynamo Kiev beat Ferencvaros (3–0) in Basle
1976	Anderlecht beat West Ham U. (4–2) in Brussels
1977	S.V. Hamburg beat Anderlecht (2–0) in Amsterdam
1978	Anderlecht beat Austria/W.A.C. (4–0) in Paris
1979	Barcelona beat Fortuna Dusseldorf (4–3, a.e.t.) in Basle
1980	Valencia beat Arsenal (0–0, a.e.t.) in Brussels (Valencia won 5–4 on penalties)
1981	Dynamo Tbilisi beat Carl Zeiss Jena (2–1) in Dusseldorf
1982	Barcelona beat Standard Liège (2–1) in Barcelona
1983	Aberdeen beat Real Madrid (2–1) in Gothenburg
1984	Juventus beat Porto (2-1) in Basle

EUROPEAN FAIRS CUP FINALS

1958	Barcelona beat London (2–2, 6–0)
1960	Barcelona beat Birmingham City (0–0, 4–1)
1961	A.S. Roma beat Birmingham City (2–2, 2–0)
1962	Valencia beat Barcelona (6–2, 1–1)
1963	Valencia beat Dynamo Zagreb (2–1, 2–0)
1964	Real Zaragoza beat Valencia (2–1) in Barcelona
1965	Ferencvaros beat Juventus (1–0) in Turin
1966	Barcelona beat Real Zaragoza (0–1, 4–2)
1967	Dynamo Zagreb beat Leeds United (2–0, 0–0)
1968	Leeds United beat Ferencvaros (1–0, 0–0)
1969	Newcastle United beat Ujpest Dozsa (3–0, 3–2)
1970	Arsenal beat Anderlecht (1–3, 3–0)
1971	Leeds United beat Juventus (2–2, 1–1, on away goals)

U.E.F.A. CUP FINALS

1972	Tottenham Hotspur beat Wolverhampton Wanderers (2–1, 1–1)
1973	Liverpool beat Borussia Moenchengladbach (3–0, 0–2)
1974	Feyenoord beat Tottenham Hotspur (2–2, 2–0)
1975	Borussia Moenchengladbach beat Tirente Enschede (0–0, 5–1)
1976	Liverpool beat Bruges (3–2, 1–1)
1977	Juventus beat Atletico Bilbao (1–0, 1–2, on away goals)
1978	P.S.V. Eindhoven beat Bastia (0–0, 3–0)
1979	Borussia Moenchengladbach beat Red Star Belgrade (1–1, 1–0)
1980	Eintracht Frankfurt beat Borussia Moenchengladbach (2–3, 1–0, on away goals)
1981	Ipswich Town beat A.Z. 67 Alkmaar (3–0, 2–4)
1982	I.F.K. Gothenburg beat S.V. Hamburg (1–0, 3–0)
1983	Anderlecht beat Benfica (1–0, 1–1)
1984	Tottenham Hotspur beat Anderlecht (1-1, 1-1; 4-3 on penalties)

The European Cup.

The Football Association Challenge Cup

The F.A. Cup was the idea of C. W. Alcock, the Secretary of the Football Association, who proposed the idea at a meeting on 20 July 1871. Alcock played in the first final in 1872, for the winners, Wanderers. Fifteen teams took part, and 2,000 watched the final at the Kennington Oval. In 1981 Tottenham Hotspur won the 100th final after a replay.

F.A. CUP FINAL RESULTS

1872	Wanderers beat Royal Engineers (1–0)
1873	Wanderers beat Oxford University (2–0)
1874	Oxford University beat Royal Engineers (2–0)
1875	Royal Engineers beat Old Etonians (2–0 after 1–1 draw)
1876	Wanderers beat Old Etonians (3–0 after 1–1 draw)
1877	Wanderers beat Oxford University (2–1 a.e.t.)
1878	Wanderers beat Royal Engineers (3–1)
1879	Old Etonians beat Clapham Rovers (1–0)
1880	Clapham Rovers beat Oxford University (1–0)
1881	Old Carthusians beat Old Etonians (3–0)
1882	Old Etonians beat Blackburn R. (1–0)
1883	Blackburn Olympic beat Old Etonians (2–1 a.e.t.)
1884	Blackburn R. beat Queen's Park, Glasgow (2–1)
1885	Blackburn R. beat Queen's Park, Glasgow (2–0)
1886	Blackburn R. beat W.B.A. (2–0 after 0–0 draw)
1887	Aston Villa beat W.B.A. (2–0)
1888	W.B.A. beat Preston North End (2–1)
1889	Preston North End beat Wolverhampton W. (3–0)
1890	Blackburn R. beat Sheffield W. (6–1)
1891	Blackburn R. beat Notts County (3–1)
1892	W.B.A beat Aston Villa (3–0)
1893	Wolverhampton W. beat Everton (1–0)
1894	Notts County beat Bolton W. (4–1)
1895	Aston Villa beat W.B.A. (1–0)
1896	Sheffield W. beat Wolverhampton W. (2–1)
1897	Aston Villa beat Everton (3–2)
1898	Nottingham F. beat Derby County (3–1)
1899	Sheffield U. beat Derby County (4–1)
1900	Bury beat Southampton (4–0)
1901	Tottenham H. beat Sheffield U. (3–1 after 2–2 draw)
1902	Sheffield U. beat Southampton (2–1 after 1–1 draw)
1903	Bury beat Derby County (6–0)
1904	Manchester C. beat Bolton W. (1–0)
1905	Aston Villa beat Newcastle U. (2–0)
1906	Everton beat Newcastle U. (1–0)
1907	Sheffield W. beat Everton (2–1)
1908	Wolverhampton W. beat Newcastle U. (3–1)
1909	Manchester U. beat Bristol C. (1–0)
1910	Newcastle U. beat Barnsley (2–0 after 1–1 draw)
1911	Bradford C. beat Newcastle U. (1–0 after 0–0 draw)
1912	Barnsley beat W.B.A. (1–0 a.e.t., after 0–0 draw)
1913	Aston Villa beat Sunderland (1–0)
1914	Burnley beat Liverpool (1–0)
1915	Sheffield U. beat Chelsea (3–0)
1920	Aston Villa beat Huddersfield T. (1–0 a.e.t.)
1921	Tottenham·H. beat Wolverhampton W. (1–0)
1922	Huddersfield T. beat Preston North End (1–0)
1923	Bolton W. beat West Ham U. (2–0)
1924	Newcastle U. beat Aston Villa (2–0)
1925	Sheffield U. beat Cardiff C. (1–0)
1926	Bolton W. beat Manchester C. (1–0)
1927	Cardiff C. beat Arsenal (1–0)
1928	Blackburn R. beat Huddersfield T. (3–1)
1929	Bolton W. beat Portsmouth (2–0)
1930	Arsenal beat Huddersfield T. (2–0)
1931	W.B.A. beat Birmingham (2–1)
1932	Newcastle U. beat Arsenal (2–1)
1933	Everton beat Manchester C. (3–0)
1934	Manchester C. beat Portsmouth (2–1)
1935	Sheffield W. beat W.B.A. (4–2)
1936	Arsenal beat Sheffield U. (1–0)
1937	Sunderland beat Preston North End (3–1)
1938	Preston North End beat Huddersfield T. (1–0 a.e.t.)
1939	Portsmouth beat Wolverhampton W. (4–1)
1946	Derby County beat Charlton Ath. (4–1 a.e.t.)
1947	Charlton Ath. beat Burnley (1–0 a.e.t.)
1948	Manchester U. beat Blackpool (4–2)
1949	Wolverhampton W. beat Leicester C. (3–1)
1950	Arsenal beat Liverpool (2–0)
1951	Newcastle U. beat Blackpool (2–0)
1952	Newcastle U. beat Arsenal (1–0)
1953	Blackpool beat Bolton W. (4–3)
1954	W.B.A. beat Preston North End (3–2)
1955	Newcastle U. beat Manchester C. (3–1)
1956	Manchester C. beat Birmingham C. (3–1)
1957	Aston Villa beat Manchester U. (2–1)
1958	Bolton W. beat Manchester U. (2–0)
1959	Nottingham F. beat Luton T. (2–1)
1960	Wolverhampton W. beat Blackburn R. (3–0)
1961	Tottenham H. beat Leicester C. (2–0)
1962	Tottenham H. beat Burnley (3–1)
1963	Manchester U. beat Leicester C. (3–1)
1964	West Ham U. beat Preston North End (3–2)
1965	Liverpool beat Leeds U. (2–1 a.e.t.)
1966	Everton beat Sheffield W. (3–2)
1967	Tottenham H. beat Chelsea (2–1)
1968	W.B.A. beat Everton (1–0 a.e.t.)
1969	Manchester C. beat Leicester C. (1–0)
1970	Chelsea beat Leeds U. (2–1 a.e.t., after 2–2 draw a.e.t.)
1971	Arsenal beat Liverpool (2–1 a.e.t.)
1972	Leeds U. beat Arsenal (1–0)
1973	Sunderland beat Leeds U. (1–0)
1974	Liverpool beat Newcastle U. (3–0)
1975	West Ham U. beat Fulham (2–0)
1976	Southampton beat Manchester U. (1–0)
1977	Manchester U. beat Liverpool (2–1)
1978	Ipswich T. beat Arsenal (1–0)
1979	Arsenal beat Manchester U. (3–2)
1980	West Ham U. beat Arsenal (1–0)
1981	Tottenham H. beat Manchester C. (3–2, after 1–1 draw a.e.t.)
1982	Tottenham·H. beat Q.P.R. (1–0, after 1–1 draw a.e.t.)
1983	Manchester U. beat Brighton (4–0, after 2–2 draw a.e.t.)
1984	Everton beat Watford (2–0)

The Scottish Cup

The Scottish Cup, first held in 1873–74, was at first a secondary competition to the F.A. Cup, in which Scottish teams were eligible to take part. There were 16 teams entered in the first tournament, won by Scotland's oldest club, Queen's Park.

There was much argument and bitterness among Scottish clubs in the first few years, and Vale of Leven won in 1879 after Rangers had refused to replay, and Queen's Park won in 1884 when Vale of Leven declined to turn up for the final.

In 1909, a full-scale riot after two draws between Celtic and Rangers in the final caused the Scottish F.A. to withhold the Cup for that year.

SCOTTISH F.A. CUP FINALS

1874 Queen's Park beat Clydesdale (2–0)
1875 Queen's Park beat Renton (3–0)
1876 Queen's Park beat Third Lanark (2–0, after 1–1 draw)
1877 Vale of Leven beat Rangers (3–2, after 0–0 and 1–1 draws)
1878 Vale of Leven beat Third Lanark (1–0)
1879 Vale of Leven beat Rangers (Vale of Leven awarded Cup – Rangers failed to appear for replay after 1–1 draw)
1880 Queen's Park beat Thornliebank (3–0)
1881 Queen's Park beat Dumbarton (3–1, after Dumbarton protested the first game which Queen's Park won 2–1)
1882 Queen's Park beat Dumbarton (4–1, after 2–2 draw)
1883 Dumbarton beat Vale of Leven (2–1, after 2–2 draw)
1884 Queen's Park beat Vale of Leven (Queen's Park awarded the cup after Vale of Leven failed to appear)
1885 Renton beat Vale of Leven (3–1, after 0–0 draw)
1886 Queen's Park beat Renton (3–1)
1887 Hibernian beat Dumbarton (2–1)
1888 Renton beat Cambuslang (6–1)
1889 Third Lanark beat Celtic (2–1; replay by order of Scottish F.A. because of playing conditions in first match, won 3–0 by Third Lanark)
1890 Queen's Park beat Vale of Leven (2–1, after 1–1 draw)
1891 Hearts beat Dumbarton (1–0)
1892 Celtic beat Queen's Park (5–1, after mutual protested game which Celtic won 1–0)
1893 Queen's Park beat Celtic (2–1)
1894 Rangers beat Celtic (3–1)
1895 St Bernard's beat Renton (2–1)
1896 Hearts beat Hibernian (3–1)
1897 Rangers beat Dumbarton (5–1)
1898 Rangers beat Kilmarnock (2–0)
1899 Celtic beat Rangers (2–0)
1900 Celtic beat Queen's Park (4–3)
1901 Hearts beat Celtic (4–3)
1902 Hibernian beat Celtic (1–0)
1903 Rangers beat Hearts (2–0, after 1–1 and 0–0 draws)
1904 Celtic beat Rangers (3–2)
1905 Third Lanark beat Rangers (3–1, after 0–0 draw)
1906 Hearts beat Third Lanark (1–0)
1907 Celtic beat Hearts (3–0)
1908 Celtic beat St Mirren (5–1)
1909 Owing to riot the Cup was withheld after two drawn games between Celtic and Rangers (2–2 and 1–1)
1910 Dundee beat Clyde (2–1, after 2–2 and 0–0 draws)
1911 Celtic beat Hamilton A. (2–0, after 0–0 draw)
1912 Celtic beat Clyde (2–0)
1913 Falkirk beat Raith R. (2–0)
1914 Celtic beat Hibernian (4–1, after 0–0 draw)
1920 Kilmarnock beat Albion R. (3–2)
1921 Partick T. beat Rangers (1–0)
1922 Morton beat Rangers (1–0)
1923 Celtic beat Hibernian (1–0)

1924 Airdrieonians beat Hibernian (2–0)
1925 Celtic beat Dundee (2–1)
1926 St Mirren beat Celtic (2–0)
1927 Celtic beat East Fife (3–1)
1928 Rangers beat Celtic (4–0)
1929 Kilmarnock beat Rangers (2–0)
1930 Rangers beat Partick T. (2–0, after 0–0 draw)
1931 Celtic beat Motherwell (4–2, after 2–2 draw)
1932 Rangers beat Kilmarnock (3–0, after 1–1 draw)
1933 Celtic beat Motherwell (1–0)
1934 Rangers beat St Mirren (5–0)
1935 Rangers beat Hamilton A. (2–1)
1936 Rangers beat Third Lanark (1–0)
1937 Celtic beat Aberdeen (2–1)
1938 East Fife beat Kilmarnock (4–2, after 1–1 draw)
1939 Clyde beat Motherwell (4–0)
1947 Aberdeen beat Hibernian (2–1, after 1–1 draw)
1948 Rangers beat Morton (1–0, after 1–1 draw)
1949 Rangers beat Clyde (4–1)
1950 Rangers beat East Fife (3–0)
1951 Celtic beat Motherwell (1–0)
1952 Motherwell beat Dundee (4–0)
1953 Rangers beat Aberdeen (1–0, after 1–1 draw)
1954 Celtic beat Aberdeen (2–1)
1955 Clyde beat Celtic (1–0, after 1–1 draw)
1956 Hearts beat Celtic (3–1)
1957 Falkirk beat Kilmarnock (2–1, after 1–1 draw)
1958 Clyde beat Hibernian (1–0)
1959 St Mirren beat Aberdeen (3–1)
1960 Rangers beat Kilmarnock (2–0)
1961 Dunfermline Ath. beat Celtic (2–0, after 0–0 draw)
1962 Rangers beat St Mirren (2–0)
1963 Rangers beat Celtic (3–0, after 1–1 draw)
1964 Rangers beat Dundee (3–1)
1965 Celtic beat Dunfermline Ath. (3–2)
1966 Rangers beat Celtic (1–0, after 0–0 draw)
1967 Celtic beat Aberdeen (2–0)
1968 Dunfermline Ath. beat Hearts (3–1)
1969 Celtic beat Rangers (4–0)
1970 Aberdeen beat Celtic (3–1)
1971 Celtic beat Rangers (2–1, after 1–1 draw)
1972 Celtic beat Hibernian (6–1)
1973 Rangers beat Celtic (3–2)
1974 Celtic beat Dundee U. (3–0)
1975 Celtic beat Airdrieonians (3–1)
1976 Rangers beat Hearts (3–1)
1977 Celtic beat Rangers (1–0)
1978 Rangers beat Aberdeen (2–1)
1979 Rangers beat Hibernian (3–2, after 0–0 and 0–0 draws)
1980 Celtic beat Rangers (1–0)
1981 Rangers beat Dundee U. (4–1, after 0–0 draw)
1982 Aberdeen beat Rangers (4–1 a.e.t.)
1983 Aberdeen beat Rangers (1–0 a.e.t.)
1984 Aberdeen beat Celtic (2–1)

Some Great Players of Past and Present

Osvaldo Ardiles gained a world-wide reputation with his displays for Argentina in the 1978 World Cup finals. Shortly afterwards he joined Tottenham Hotspur and made an immediate impact in the English First Division. He announced an ambition to win an F.A. Cup winners' medal to accompany his World Cup winners' medal, and achieved this in 1981. In 1982 he joined Paris Saint-Germain on loan from Spurs, returning to Spurs again in 1983.

Gordon Banks was voted the best goalkeeper in the 1966 World Cup in which he won a winners' medal with England. When he made a fantastic save from Pelé in the 1970 World Cup finals, it was repeated on television playbacks around the world and he was universally considered the world's best. In 1972 he suffered an eye injury in a car crash that cut short his career, but a goalkeeping record of 73 caps for England and his World Cup feats ensure his reputation as one of the best ever.

George Best never played in the World Cup finals, but he is still recognized as one of the best post-war footballers. Born in Belfast, he made his first appearance for Manchester United when 17 in 1962 and was immediately seen to be a footballing genius. He was afforded pop-star status and the pressure of his popularity led to a life style which frequently caused him trouble with his club. On the field he won a European Cup winners' medal and 37 caps for Northern Ireland. His exciting dribbling, and his speed and flair as a winger, made him unforgettable to those who saw him in his prime.

John Charles was a magnificently built footballer of 1.35 m. (6 ft. 1 in.) with immense strength. He was also very skilful and never needed to use his physique unfairly. He was known as 'the Gentle Giant' at Leeds United and '*Il Buon Gigante*' during his spell with Juventus in Italy. Born in Swansea, he was perhaps the best of all Welsh players, with great heading ability, and he won 38 caps at centre and inside-forward and at centre-half.

Bobby Charlton survived the Munich air disaster of 1958 which killed so many of his colleagues in the great Manchester United side. He became one of England's best-loved footballers and a great ambassador for the game all round the world. An attacking midfield player, his most famous asset was a thundering shot, which brought him a record 49 goals for England in 106 internationals. Apart from 1974-75 as player-manager of Preston, he played only for Manchester United, winning a European Cup winner's medal in 1968 to add to his 1966 World Cup winner's medal.

Osvaldo Ardilles dribbling for Argentina.

Johan Cruyff was born near the Ajax stadium in Amsterdam, Holland where he won many honours, including three European Cup medals. On the retirement of Pelé, he was accepted as the world's best footballer. He was a marvellous attacking forward with amazing ball control and acceleration. He was part of a football renaissance in Holland and captained the national team in the World Cup Final of 1974. This they unluckily lost, although around this time Holland was arguably the best footballing nation in the world. After a spell in the United States, he returned to Holland to play for Feyenoord in 1983.

Kenny Dalglish joined Liverpool from Celtic in 1977 and became known as 'King of the Kop'. His skill at making sharp turns and shielding the ball in the penalty area has led to many goals for himself and others. By 1983 he had played for Scotland a record 90 times, and appeared in three World Cup final tournaments.

Alfredo Di Stefano was born in Barracas, Argentina. He played in Argentina and Colombia before signing for Real Madrid in Spain in 1954. He then led one of the best club sides to victory in the first five European Cup competitions, and was widely considered to be the most complete footballer in the World. He played as a deep-lying centre-forward, the organizer of the team. He won seven caps for Argentina and 31 for Spain.

Tom Finney, the choice of some as England's greatest footballer, had to wait until after the war to make an impact on the soccer scene. Best as a winger, he played 76 times for England in four forward positions and scored 30 goals, then a record. He also scored nearly 250 goals in 565 games for Preston. With superb ball control and great speed he was mainly responsible for Preston being in the First Division from 1951 to 1960.

Trevor Francis was a goal-scorer from his first appearance for Birmingham City at the age of 16. In 1979 he was the subject of the first British £1 million transfer when he joined Nottingham Forest, and after another to Manchester City, he went to Sampdoria in Italy for £1.2 million in 1982. He is England's most dangerous attacker and by 1983 had won 40 caps.

Kenny Dalglish chips the ball for Liverpool against Manchester City.

Johan Cruyff, Holland's master striker in action.

Jimmy Greaves was England's best post-war goal scorer. Born in Dagenham, Essex, he made his debut for Chelsea in 1957, scoring a brilliant equalizer. He was to retain the happy knack of scoring on his debut for each new club and at all levels of football. He went to A.C. Milan in 1961 and was transferred to Spurs a year later. He achieved his goal-scoring feats from inside-forward by stealth, anticipation, coolness and brilliant ball control. In 495 Football League matches, all in the First Division, he scored 357 goals. Altogether he scored 492, including 44 for England (second to Bobby Charlton) in 57 matches.

Johnny Haynes was born in London. He became the Football League's first £100-a-week man and played 594 League games for his only club, Fulham. He became, at inside-forward, the club's general and the most accurate and imaginative passer of a ball in soccer. He played 56 times for England, 22 as captain.

Pat Jennings was born in Newry, Northern Ireland, and is well-known for his large hands and spectacular one-handed saves. He joined Watford as a goalkeeper in 1963 then joined Spurs in 1964 where he won many honours and international caps before being transferred to Arsenal in 1977. His career was crowned with appearances in the World Cup finals of 1982, and in 1983 he played his 100th game for Northern Ireland, a record.

Kevin Keegan had a brilliant honours-winning career with Liverpool, culminating in a European Cup winners' medal in 1977. He then joined S.V. Hamburg, twice being voted European Footballer of the Year, before returning to England, playing for Southampton in 1980 and going to Newcastle in 1982. A fine goal-scoring inside-forward he played part of a match as a substitute in the 1982 World Cup finals, but was not included in new manager Bobby Robson's first team thereafter. He had played 63 times for England, often as captain.

Denis Law became Scotland's youngest-ever international footballer in 1958 at 18 years and 7 months

Pat Jennings frustrates an attack by Sheffield United.

old. An inside-forward with skill and daring in the penalty area, his explosive scoring headers were his hallmark. His main club was Manchester United with whom he won many honours, and he played 55 times for Scotland scoring 30 goals.

Tommy Lawton was born in Bolton, England. The war interrupted his career, but in international football he averaged a goal a game: 22 in 23 games, or 46 in 45 if unofficial wartime matches are included. He was a superb header, and regarded as one of the best centre-forwards the game has ever seen. Playing mainly for Everton, Chelsea, Notts County and Arsenal, he scored 231 League goals.

Diego Maradona burst upon the international soccer scene in 1979 and was quickly regarded as the most exciting player in the World. An inside-forward with speed and skill, he had already won 33 caps for Argentina by the end of the 1982 World Cup finals. He began with Argentinos Juniors and Boca Juniors, but in 1982 joined Barcelona in Spain for a world record fee of £4 million. Hepatitis followed by an ankle injury after a bad tackle kept him out of the game for some months in his first season in Spain.

Sir Stanley Matthews is perhaps the most famous of pre-war footballers. He made his debut for Stoke in 1931 and was nicknamed the 'Wizard of Dribble' for his trickery on the right wing. A fitness fanatic, he continued playing till 1964-65, when he was 50. Perhaps the highlight of his career came in 1953 when, playing for Blackpool, he was brilliant in a 4-3 Cup-Final win in a match known as 'Matthews' match'. He played 698 League matches and won 54 full caps plus making 26 wartime appearances for England. He was knighted in 1965.

Bobby Moore had an almost perfect career, joining West Ham United from school, leading them to F.A. Cup and European Cup Winners Cup successes and then, in 1966, captaining England's winning side in the World Cup. He was still only 25. He played on the left-hand side of the defence, rarely lost a tackle and led his teams by example, with cool constructive play. He went on to win a record 108 caps for England.

Gerhard Muller, a short stocky centre-forward with immensely powerful legs, was brilliant at snatching goals in the penalty area. Quick to turn, deadly in shot and powerful with his head, he enjoyed success with Bayern Munich (four European medals) and West Germany (World Cup and European Championship medals). In 62 internationals he scored 68 goals, 14 in the World Cup finals of 1970 and 1974.

Pelé, the most famous footballer of all, was born Edson Arantas do Nascimento in Tres Coracoes, Brazil. A complete attacking player, he was first noticed by the World when he scored a brilliant goal in the 1958

Georgios Koudas of Greece tries to intercept Bobby Moore.

World Cup final, when only 17. He played in the World Cup finals of 1962 and 1966, and had another brilliant tournament in Brazil's win in 1970. He won numerous medals with his club, Santos, played at the end of his career for New York Cosmos, and, in all, scored over 1,200 goals, 97 in 110 matches for Brazil.

Ferenc Puskas was known as 'The Galloping Major'. He was a chubby inside-forward, and in 1953 came to England with the Hungarian side which inflicted the first home defeat (6-3) on England by a foreign side. Hungary were the best team in the World, and Puskas, with his tremendous left foot shooting, was their best player. He fled Hungary during the uprising of 1956 and played for Real Madrid, in Spain, winning a European Cup winners medal. He scored 85 goals in 84 games for Hungary, and also played four times for Spain.

Bryan Robson became Britain's most expensive player when he was transferred from West Bromwich Albion to Manchester United for £1.5 million in 1981. A strong midfield player, he has a mastery of all aspects of the game, including scoring vital goals. He first appeared for England in 1980, and by 1983 had won 27 caps and established himself as captain.

Paolo Rossi was born in Prato, Italy. He was one of the Italian successes in the 1978 World Cup finals, but half way through the 1979–80 season was banned for

two years for being implicated in the betting and bribery scandal that rocked Italian soccer. He came back just in time to play centre-forward for Italy in the 1982 World Cup finals, and won a winners' medal. He was the finals' top scorer with six goals, including a hat-trick against Brazil.

Karl-Heinz Rummenigge was born in Lippstadt, West Germany, and was European Footballer of the Year twice in the 1980s. He joined Bayern Munich in 1974 and obtained a European Cup winners' medal in 1976. A dribbling, goal-scoring winger, he gained his 59th cap in the 1982 World Cup Final.

Marco Tardelli was born in Lucca, Italy, joined Juventus in 1975 and by the beginning of the 1982–83 soccer season had played 62 times for Italy. A midfield player, he was regarded in soccer as a hard destroyer, regularly being sent off for fouls. However, in the 1982 World Cup Final, Tardelli proved that he could be a complete all-round footballer, scored a goal and was the official 'man of the match'.

Dino Zoff is a goalkeeper who captained Italy 40 times, including the World Cup victory in 1982. He was born Mariano del Friuli, and was the only player to play in both Italy's European Nations Cup win in 1968 and the World Cup in 1982. In 1973 and 1974 he kept a clean sheet for Italy for 1,143 minutes of football. His 106 caps for Italy are a record for his country.

Tactics

From the diagrams you have seen so far in this book, you will realise something of the tactical possibilities open to the player who keeps his eyes open. At the very front of this book you will find a pitch diagram. Cut round the players as shown, glue your cut-outs to buttons, and place them on the pitch. You can now demonstrate what you have learnt to your team mates. Before you play, use the cut-outs to devise new tactics you can use; after the game you can use them to show where you went wrong! Try setting up the players in different team formations. At the back of the book you will see the various possibilities.

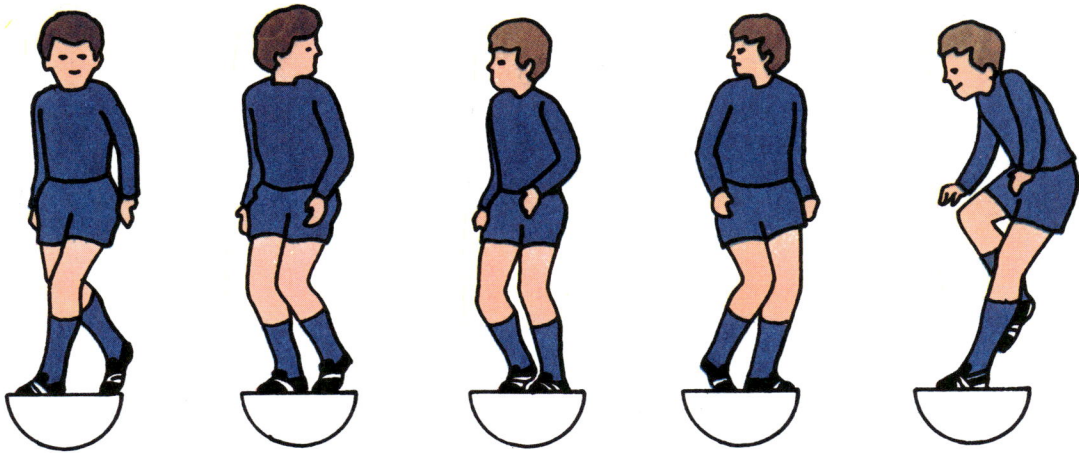

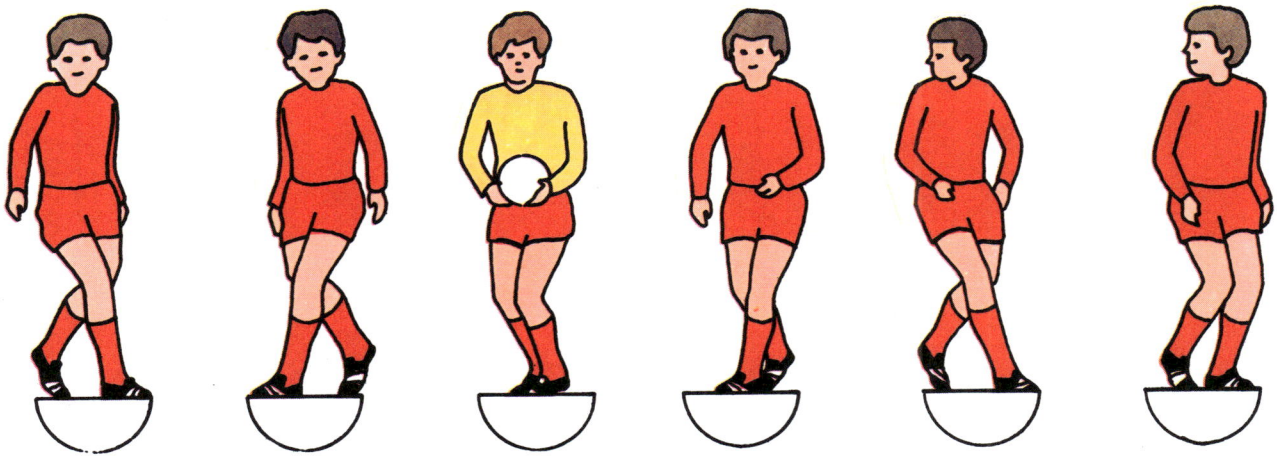

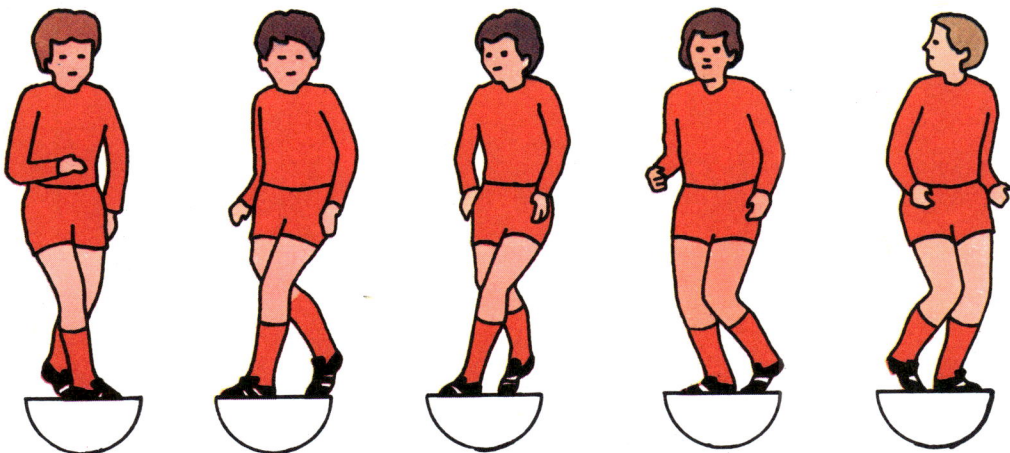

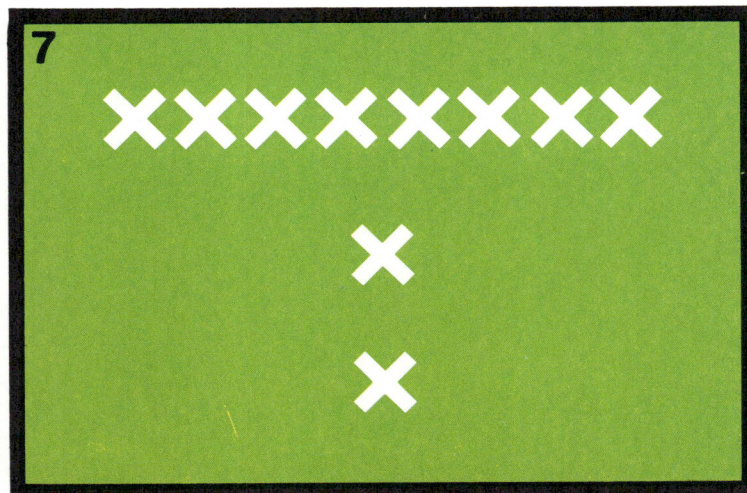

1: 4–4–2
formation as used by England to win the 1966 World Cup

2: 4–3–3
formation as used by Brazil to win the 1970 World Cup

3: 4–2–4
formation used by Brazil to win the World Cup in 1958 and 1962

4: The W formation, the traditional line-up of the 1930's, 1940's and early 1950's. The two old-fashioned inside forwards dropped slightly behind the centre forward and wingers, and the centre half dropped back between the fullbacks.

5: The 2–3–5 formation used from the 1890's until the offside law was changed in 1925. Two backs, three half-backs and five forwards with the centre-half in an attacking roll in support of his forward and the wing-halves playing wide near the touchlines and marking the opposing wingers.

6: The 2–2–6 formation used in the mid-1880's.

7: And finally 1–1–8 from the days when tactics and defensive ideas were in their infancy, and nearly every player just chased the ball!

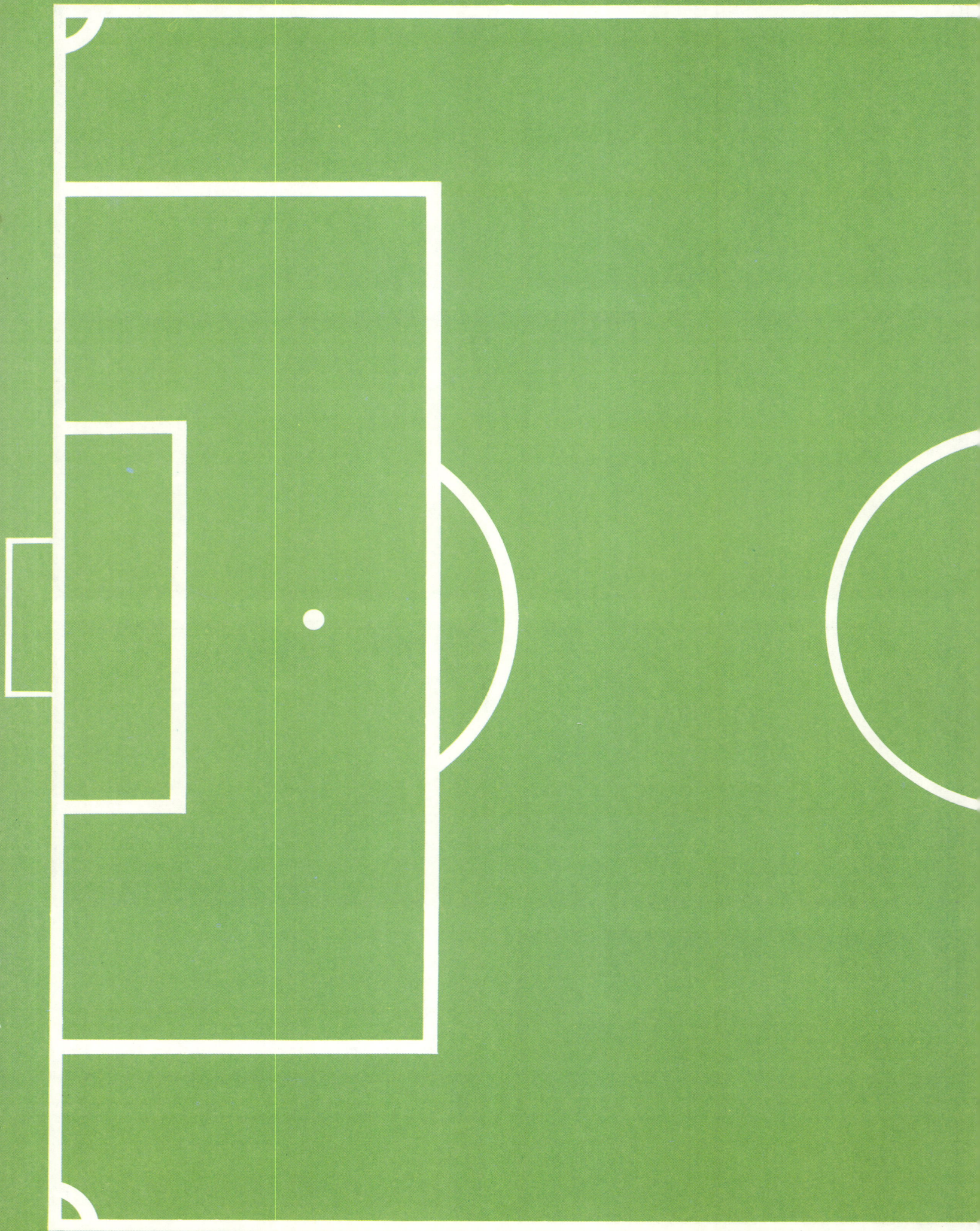